# Simple Fly Life:  The Manual

Also by Amity Collatt Farr

*Minimize: Kill your debt. Live your dream.*

*Minimize: The Great Interior*

*Minimize: Cents for Kids*

*Follow Simple Fly Life on Facebook and simpleflylife.com*

Simple Fly Life: The Manual

by Amity Collatt Farr

KDP Publishing

Copyright 2018; 2020. Amity Collatt Farr all rights reserved

Disclaimers:

The advice in this book is not intended to take the place of professional counseling.

For everyone who wants to taste freedom in their life

# Acknowledgements

A heartfelt thank-you goes to:

Jesus, for allowing me the fun of making four books and going into a business about which I am passionate.

My awesome parents, Jim and Marilyn Murrow, for their editing and proofreading contributions.

CJ, my dear husband, for his tireless support and giving me the freedom to pursue this project on my terms. He is also the designer of the graphics of the original cover.

Cynthia Reeves of Game Ink Design for the brilliant cover, and Jan Farr for the original photo credits.

Thanks also to Tara Kirby and Elizabeth Ripper for their wonderful contributions to the chapter on life and decluttering with kids. You made this book much more than it could have been otherwise. Also, thanks to Tara and Elizabeth for reading the manuscript and giving feedback and suggestions to make it better.

Thank you to all who have supported me in my minimizing. To those that never laughed at it and encouraged me to pursue my dreams, I appreciate you.

# Simple Fly Life:
# Table of Contents

## The Internal Job

| | |
|---|---|
| 9 | Introduction |
| 15 | The Sermon |
| 24 | My Story |
| 35 | Philosophy 101 |
| 44 | Benefits |
| 55 | Day of Reconciliation |
| 63 | Introduction to Decluttering |

## Outward Manifestations

| | |
|---|---|
| 69 | How to Eat an Elephant: Purging |
| 79 | Offloading Stuff |
| 88 | Time Management |
| 97 | The Lazy Budget |
| 108 | Spending Fasts |
| 113 | Media Fasts |
| 119 | The Sketch-Journal |
| 124 | Vision Setting |
| 131 | Authenticity |
| 139 | Sharing |

| | |
|---|---|
| 145 | Gratitude |
| 155 | Involve God |

## On The Journey

| | |
|---|---|
| 163 | Spouses, Significant Others, and Roommates |
| 169 | Kids and Decluttering |
| 186 | Barriers |
| 192 | Seven Deadly Sins for Simplifying |
| 197 | Life after Debt |
| 207 | The Last Word |

## Afterthoughts

| | |
|---|---|
| 210 | The Frugal Way |
| 226 | The Playbook |
| 251 | More From Amity's Other Books… |

# Introduction

"Something" is devouring our spaces, time, money, energy, and talent. We have endless dust collecting on knickknacks lining our shelves; and we can't recall why we bought the majority of them. And, frankly, don't even like a majority of them when we are honest with ourselves.

We have more clothes than hangers and haven't worn a lot of our outfits for a very long time. Our closets may be walk-in closets in theory, but are packed to the brim with a tiny walkway through its depths. Stacks of various and sundry goods are spilling off the closet shelves in every room that has a storage feature. The attic and basement haven't been touched for a good cleaning and inventory since Truman was in office.

We don't have enough; we have excess. We are miserable in our messes. Some of us (and, we know who we are), even pay a hefty, monthly storage fee to rent a commercial storage unit, or have a shed packed to the gills as a monument to our consumption in our back yards. They aren't cheap, or pretty.

So why are we doing this to ourselves?

Here is a typical American life snapshot: We are drowning in stuff. We are swarmed with obligations imposed by our jobs, others, and egos. We are chained to our jobs by our bills. We just exist. We are overwhelmed, stressed, chronically depressed, and anxious. We are imprisoned in our circumstances from the debt generated by our choices to finance our couch, digital assistance, car, education, and house. Not to mention, we are buying slavery through our subscriptions to cable, audiobooks, magazines, and the notion that a fancy coffee is a better coffee.

If we are honest with ourselves, we will admit that our health and happiness are fading memories. Not to give up, we buy, buy, buy hoping for our bliss to return to us. Our money doesn't cover our outgo, and our intake is astonishing and grotesquely out of proportion to the rest of the world's consumption. We are not thriving; rather, we are slowly dying inside while our bank accounts dwindle and go in the red.

Consider this: In 1940, according to newser.com, the average house was 1,177 square feet. In 2010, that had swelled to 2,392 square feet - for the average home, not some grand castle on a hill.[1]

Also, during that time, 48% of family sizes reduced from four children in 1940 to two in 2010.[2]

What was the incentive and logic for doubling space in light of shrinking families? Stuff. We needed more space for stuff. We added mud rooms, dens, media rooms, personal gyms, and home theaters as well as large laundry rooms.

But, did we really require more stuff and space to put it, when we had fewer humans to shelter and fewer needs for the space? That we wanted more space and many more things is obvious. Now that we have it, we struggle to save a dime for retirement and emergencies.

Our sense of personal peace is undone by all the laundry that is billowing out of our bedrooms and bathrooms. Our DVD collection (which we have not bothered to shelve again after pilfering through it to find a title to alleviate boredom) roosts on our entertainment centers and floors, adding a little deviation from classiness in our dwellings.

It's a small wonder then, that we are overly stressed. That's actually high risk for losing everything. Medical emergencies, retirement crises, and economic recessions are high risks when we are stretched so thinly.

As my veteran father would point out, like a combat team in hostile territory, it isn't *if* there is an attack, (economic disasters, job loss, and medical emergencies); rather, it is when. The only variables are: when and how high (tragic) the losses will be when the dust settles.

If you are still pondering whether we really are drowning in stuff, and are losing our way in life, consider these startling (and typical) revelations from a survey of 1,000 American women by ClosetMaid:

- "women only really like ten percent of their wardrobe."
- "one in ten women are depressed when they open their closet"
- "40 percent of women state they don't like any of their clothes."[3]

Furthermore, in 2018's World Happiness Report, the United States came in 18th out of 156 countries surveyed. Surprising, when we think we have it so good in America with our never-ending bounty and consumption of luxuries and resources.[4]

So, what is going on? We have increased the size of our homes, have multiple outfits hanging in our walk-ins, put ourselves in hock for almost everything we own; and we are not even in the top ten happiest countries in the world. What gives, and how can we get out of this mess?

Like the warriors that fought alongside my father in Vietnam, we need plenty of the right ammo, intel, and discipline. Our war is not against flesh and blood, but against encroaching over-consumption and greed that leads to misery, debt, and despair.

This book is designed to introduce you to the tools, philosophy, and kick-in-the-pants needed to start clearing a swath through the mess surrounding you. You can have victory and supremely sought-after benefits: more time, more money, and less stress. You will learn how to simplify in these pages - to get rid of the things that don't matter, to make room for the things that do. You will start building a healthier financial future with what you need and really want in life.

Come with me on a journey out of the madness. I won't tell you to do things that didn't work for me, and that I haven't done, or don't do for myself. I have been on this journey for almost nine years now; and I am a poster child for the game-changing power of simplifying. Pick up this book, turn the pages, and learn about a lifestyle and its practical application that can set you free.

Go ahead and dig into this manual. Your dream life is waiting!

1. http://www.newser.com/story/225645/average-size-of-us-homes-decade-by-decade.html

2. (Gad,G.,2018, Pew research System)

3. http://www.dailymail.co.uk/femail/article-3564177/The-struggle-real-Infographic-reveals-average-woman-103-ITEMS-closet-laying-REAL-reasons-never-wear.html

4. https://en.wikipedia.org/wiki/World_Happiness_Report

# The Sermon

In my practice as a Physical Therapist Assistant, I have the opportunity to educate on decreasing the risk of falling at home. This is considered "home safety education," but to jazz it up a little, I call it my Home Safety Sermon.

I bill it to my patients as "the shortest sermon you are ever gonna' hear." That usually brings a raised eyebrow and a slight smile. The Home Safety Sermon is this:

- use nightlights
- have something on your feet with tread
- get rid of small rugs, except by the shower
- Plan your route so you have something to sit on or lean up against when you get tired - don't get stranded in a wide open place

Today you, too, shall hear a sermon (if you keep reading). It won't be as short as the one I give at work, nor is it to help prevent falls. But, it just may prevent you from having regrets at the end of your life.

* * *

How do we get to where we have abundance? Do we have abundance when we are surrounded by inanimate objects? How much money will it take for us to be satisfied?

Do you already have a dollar amount in mind that you need to make to have everything you want? What if I told you that likely you are already making enough money to have true abundance? Would you want to laugh at me? Spit a chewed-up Oreo cookie at me?

Consider this:

The secret to having abundance is not in having more, it is in desiring less. If you take two people making the exact same amount of money, and one desires less - way less - than the other, likely that person who doesn't need so much is going to feel that they have plenty on their paychecks, even if their pay is quite modest.

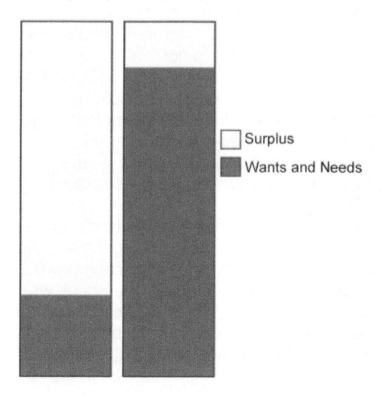

On the other hand, the person who needs to spend almost all of their income to satisfy their wants and needs is going to feel like they don't have enough. They may actually run a deficit, where they spend more than they make to get their desires placated.

Keep in mind, our two hypothetical people make the same amount. When you want what you have, you have what you want.

> When you want what you have, you have what you want.

When you desire what you have and not everything you don't have, you will have a sense of serenity and plenty and your "little" will feel like a "lot."

(Later on in this book, there will be discussions about tips and tactics to help you desire less so you can feel that abundance. We will cover mighty weapons against discontent like gratitude and media fasts. But for now, on with the sermon.)

In a wonderful book that has been revised, updated, and reprinted many times, Joe Dominguez and Vicki Robin laid out profound principles for changing your life and your outcome in finances. Their book was titled Your Money or Your Life; and I don't think you would come away from reading it without feeling inspired and uplifted, as well as a little determined.

The secret to happiness was hinted at in Joe and Vicki's writings. It could be communicated as a graph, and I have forgotten now where I have seen it exactly as I will relate it, but <u>Your Money or Your Life</u> had something very similar and poignant, and it will demystify exactly what happens to our satisfaction as we accumulate.

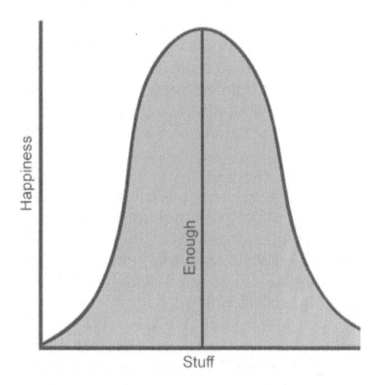

The X axis on the graph is how much stuff you have. The higher the coordinate of the X value, the more you have. The Y axis is your happiness. The higher the Y value, the more happiness you have.

At the beginning of the graph, you have hardly anything and your happiness is low. The line starts to arc up for happiness as you acquire more and more. Up, up, up goes the happiness as more desires start being met - needs and wants.

And, then, you reach the highest the arc will ever go. After the apex, the more you acquire, the lower your happiness is. Strange? Yes. But, this explains why there are so many desperately unhappy people surrounded by mounds of stuff and clutter in their homes. If having stuff was key to happiness, hoarders would be in a permanent state of ecstasy.

Then it becomes clear. The trick to happiness with stuff is to find "Enough." Throughout this book I will call enough, "The Essential." It is that magic level of stuff you can have while optimizing your happiness potential as it relates to material belongings and ownership of those belongings.

Here is a thought: everything you own, owns you. That is very true. Everything you own requires a certain amount of maintenance and upkeep, and don't forget you need to dispose of it responsibly when you finally tire of it and want to let it go!

You may think that you have stuff that serves you, like a dishwasher. But when the filter plugs up and the jets get clogged, you may realize it owns you as you have to call a service technician and use part of your precious evening or weekend to get it repaired. Perhaps you will hear the musical artist, Sting, echoing in your head: *"then you'll find your servant is your master."*

The Police's classic, "Wrapped Around Your Finger," comes to the front of my mind when I can't find my blessed car keys and I am trying to get on the road toward work. So much depth and truth is contained within that small phrase about who is really in charge.

It is as though an invisible, silken cord is attached to you from every item in your possession. That responsibility, the time and effort needed to hang on to those things, can be overwhelming.

Consider the irony of working 8-, 10-, or even 12-hour days during the week to air condition and heat trinkets, baubles, and knickknacks. Find this funny and absurd? Yet we do this, year after year, as we go to earn a paycheck to secure housing for all we bought.

Very few of us get to enjoy our homes for more than a few hours each day. Instead, we are where we don't want to be, in a job we despise and resent, while our belongings are unused and collecting bits of stardust on their surfaces. The majority of our time at home is spent sleeping (eight hours if we can come by it) and that isn't enjoying knickknacks and doodads either.

We earn more money so that we can buy more baubles. And then we have to work more to pay for those baubles and their upkeep. We lie to ourselves and tell our own souls and each other that with the next great (and often more expensive) purchase that gnawing in our spirits will be abated.

We come from a culture where "belongings" equals belonging. Our identity is wrapped up in our stuff, so we must have the right stuff to win love and acceptance. Small wonder we are so miserable.

We are up to our eyeballs in debt and discontent. Nothing we do solves the gnawing in our souls for more - more experiences, more stuff, and more accolades through choosing the right stuff.

We have homes overloaded with possessions. We are tied to a job we don't enjoy through our need for money to pay our debts and stay out of bankruptcy and ahead of the bulldozer of bills. Our time on the weekends is spent binging on TV shows and video games. We are glued to our devices while our relationships languish.

A friend with a green thumb and a unique and a fun sense of style, once told me a truth: most of us are scared of reality. She said we medicate ourselves with media - books, TV, movies, and games; and she is quite right. Our lives, if we really look hard at them, are usually terrifying. The boredom of everyday existence, coupled with unmet expectations of our own potential and lack of achievements, translates into a very unsettling reality.

Most of us cannot stand to be in the room with ourselves. Don't believe me? See if you can stand silence and solitude - just being there for minutes or hours with your own thoughts. No radio. No TV. No podcast. Just be. What happens to you?

We need to break free. The insanity of our situation needs attention: we need to look at ourselves and our situation and have an altar call to change our ways. Simplifying will be a revelation, and a start to freedom.

If you are in the middle of the conundrum that I just laid out, where you are surrounded by stuff, deeply in debt, and unhappy with your life, don't despair. You are in a position to radically change the remainder of your life and fill it with benefits and blessings untold.

How am I so sure? I was once there. Keep reading. My story is coming up, and perhaps it will resonate with you and inspire you. I have full faith that if I can better my circumstances through simplifying, you can too.

Go ahead, turn the page. And, as I tell my patients, you have just survived my sermon.

My Story

Growing up, I never felt poor. During the recession of the 1980's my parents sometimes lived on $8,000 per year. They were frugal, and could get the best value for their dollar.

When my father was a young man, his records from the Navy were lost for a year. During that time he had hardly any income. He learned how to buy groceries (in the 1960's) for seven dollars a month. He lived on things like chicken necks. He made it work, and made it edible. He is still a fantastic, inventive cook to this day. Chickens run for cover when they see him coming.

My mom raised me on a teacher's salary. I didn't get name brand clothes, certainly not the cool stuff everyone else was wearing, but I did get to go on beach vacations quite frequently as a teenager.

Once I was launched out of the house, she had enough from her savings that she built a brand new house - over 2000 square feet - and paid cash for everything. She is debt free as this book is written, and only uses debt when it fancies her to maintain her credit score. She doesn't have to, and she is methodical about it. When she gets aggravated with having payments, she pays her loans off early.

Mom was, and continues to be, marvelous at managing her money.

My mom's mother was very frugal. She was immune to TJ Maxx and could window shop all day without buying a thing. She lived very modestly throughout her entire life, and provided all her children and grandchildren a healthy inheritance.

My dad's mom also gets mentioned for her frugal streak. Grandma would reuse tea bags. In fact, she would string the used tea bags up in her kitchen until they dried out, and then they would be ready to go for a second, third, or fourth cup of tea.

So, there really wasn't a question about if I would fall far from the tree. Frugality is in my bloodline through my parents and grandparents. But, I did roll a little once I hit the ground.

As a single college student, I experimented with budgeting but could never stick with it. I had been taught by my mother how to budget, so I got the idea. Keeping receipts was relatively easy, but I would let them pile up until the task of recording my purchases seemed way too daunting. I would give up and throw my pile of receipts in the trash.

The most important decision I made during this time of my life in my finances was to not start carrying credit card debt.

While in college, my shiny new Visa card arrived at my apartment. I charged a few things on it. The bill came, and I thought I would just pay the minimum payment, and I did. The next month came with the next bill and then I saw it. The interest charges.

I was outraged and taken aback. "Never again!" I may have said with clenched fist in my humbly decorated college apartment. I meant it. I didn't let my card lapse again during school, or beyond.

When I married, in the preceding February I made CJ, my husband-to-be, track his expenses, and I did too. We got an idea about what life would be like with our expenses together, and we saw that it could work.

When we were properly hitched, I experimented more and more with different budgeting styles. I used spreadsheets, workbooks, notebooks, plain paper, and software programs until I found what I could stick with the best.

We may seem ultra virtuous, but we were also very, very naughty with our finances. We had a habit of eating out. There were times we would eat at a restaurant twice in one day, or, at least four times a week.

We ate out when we wanted. We let groceries ruin in our refrigerator. Sometimes the whole produce bin in the bottom of the fridge would go bad.

We estimate now that on average we spent $800.00 on food - and that is a conservative estimate. If we had spent just $500.00 (that is $300.00 less per month) for the first nine years of our marriage we would have saved over $32,000.00. It still makes me sick to think about it.

In addition to sending a small fortune through our digestive tracts, I was spearheading a weekly weekend adventure to TJ Maxx, Pier One, and my favorite bookstores. I had a limit as to what I spent, but I spent my limit, week after week, month after month, year after year.

In 2009 or early 2010, I was very typical. My house was filled with knickknacks that were supported by weekly shopping trips. It was not uncommon to spend hours on the weekend with retail therapy adventures in the local outlets.

We had debt for our house and we didn't have a very robust savings plan. When our HVAC system gave up the ghost we had to finance a new one. I had more than one credit card in my name at times and I was drifting through life looking for the next thing to medicate me from reality.

That was it. I was drifting. I would use daydreams to distract myself from the hard world that surrounded me. Well, I thought it was hard. It was the normal American life. I would use movies to transport me to another reality. But shopping was my favorite escape.

One night my husband and I were at Borders bookstore and I was browsing through the self-help section (because I did have an idea that something was desperately wrong with the way I was living) and I saw a book. The book didn't have an aura or halo around it; but, I was locked in on the title: <u>Secrets of Simplicity</u>. It was authored by Mary Carlomagno.

Needless to say, the book went home with me. It was a workbook format and I completed the tasks and exercises in it faithfully over the course of several weeks. Mind blown. That is what started me on the path to simplification.

I didn't throw everything away and take a no-shopping vow. It was slow. It started with giving up lattes for a week. Then, I decided to start cleaning out my house twice a year, every year.

When I started cleaning out, sometimes I would fill half of my dining room up with castoff items. As time went on, I found less and less to part with out of my possessions. (In recent times, I am lucky to get a box of stuff out of my house with a purge because I am more selective about what I buy and less goes off to the charity bin.)

Over time, I began to get control over my shopping habit. Realizing that, in six months or less, the impulse purchases would make their march out of my house, would make me pause before buying yet another whatsamadoodle at StuffMart. The weekly pilgrimages to Pier 1 and TJ Maxx slackened and finally became a thing of the past.

The eating out got checked one evening in 2013 when my husband and I were sitting on our futon, relaxing. We turned and looked at each other and almost in unison said, "We have GOT to stop eating out." That was the day that God turned us on to frugal living, and it just got bigger and better from that night.

My husband came to me one day with a brave new idea: pay off the house early. At first I was reluctant to agree - I wanted a large cash nest egg. He was adamant though, and as it turned out, very wise and perceptive, and so we began double payments on our mortgage.

I didn't get excited about seeing extra money being thrown at our house payment until about the time the principle equalled the interest. Then I began to have a barbaric, guttural feel in my voice when I would say "WE'RE PAYING DOWN THE HOUSE!!!"

In the last year of our mortgage, we paid over $41,000.00 in principal to demolish our debt. When we saw the finish line, we threw everything we had at it. Inheritances. investments. We postponed house repairs and new clothes, and in June of 2015, we paid off that sucker.

We didn't realize it at the time, but we had just given ourselves the biggest pay raise we will ever get. Our wealth rebounded, but not without a test.

Our dear elderly neighbor died shortly before we paid off our mortgage. His house went up for sale as we got our written closure to paying off our bungalow. We then had a choice: stay out of debt, or buy his house and hopefully have control over our next neighbor.

We chose wisely. We did not spring for his house, and our neighbors have been great in the rental that house became. We saw our wealth in one investment account grow over 10 times (and, I am not kidding) in two-and-a-half years from what we started with at Day One of being debt free. It was amazing. It continues to be amazing.

We re-built our emergency fund in record time. We invested regularly into our 401k's and private investments and saw healthy growth in everything. Because we were living well below our means, it was not uncommon for us to save several thousand of dollars in a month's time.

In April of 2015, we reached The Essential. This will be better explained later in this book, but it is the perfect level of stuff. Now it is 2018, and not much has changed in the volume of our house goods. We certainly don't need a bigger house, and we could downsize further from our 1100-square-foot castle, if we so needed.

Reaching The Essential and maintaining a debt-free status has opened up a new world of possibilities for us. I was able to work part-time at my job, dropping from 80 to 48 hours per pay-period. We made it work because I was available to work on frugality and running my household instead of feeling entitled to material and experiential treats because I worked full-time. We were able to save at the same amount, and sometimes even greater than previously.

My husband worked full-time for another year after I went to part-time status, but this past February he turned in his notice, without another job lined up. We could do that because we were well-padded by that time (two years after becoming debt free).

For me, I work on this project and its predecessor, Minimize Ministries. I made presentations and counseling sessions with groups and individuals in 2017, in partnership with a Health and Wellness program.

I also run a frugal household, doing things like making my own laundry detergent and shopping at discount grocery stores. To be fair, I also shop at higher-end stores, but I shop the sales. I also take care of the maintenance on the house and the vehicles, and was hiring done, what needed to be done, to take the stress off my husband while he was working full-time.

My husband uses his freedom to partner with a fellow programmer to make indie video games. He is so excited and energized to have time to work on his dream. He was so happy when he finally had time to pursue his own interests, and have less time taken being under someone else's rule. I have a happier, more engaged spouse as a result.

We did want financial independence for a long time. We still wouldn't mind it, but we are knowingly going towards working more years (we did think we could retire completely in our late 40's) so that we can have more freedom while we are young.

The grace of God brought us here, but our Creator used wisdom to bring us to the point that we embraced frugality and stopped being a couple of Captain Sillypants with our finances. Decluttering was the beginning of a revolution for both of us, and one we still benefit from greatly today.

We traded exotic vacations for extended time for coffee with the cats the majority of the mornings during the week. We traded name brand wardrobes for an abundance of time to devote to our own projects and dreams. I still have name brand clothes, but they come from thrift stores (more on that later).

I share these things because I want you to have the opportunities I have had, and perhaps even greater than these. Frugality is magical. Budgets are not shackles. Through material abstinence and financial responsibility you can live the life you can only dream about today.

Congrats on making it this far! Up next, we will take a look at truths. No worries, we aren't going to get all deep and googly-eyed talking about philosophy. But, like the Christian is transformed through embracing the truths of God, we will be renewed by realizing the lies of the culture we are in, and choosing sensible things to hold near and dear to our hearts.

Philosophy 101

There are some lies and some truths that need to be explored before getting to the nitty-gritty tools for executing simplification in your home and financial life. We will look at the lies first, and then will embrace the truths that are such a game-changer.

It starts out as a niggle in the back of your brain. "Something is not right here." There is something just out of reach. "There is something wrong with my world."

You start searching. Maybe if you buy a new sweater. "No." Perhaps if you upgrade your car. "No." The feeling of being off-center doesn't leave you.

That disconnect is precious. It is uncomfortable and frightening, but it is oh, so necessary for change. You *can* change.

The first lie that you need to rethink that you are told multiple times a day, day in, day out, is that "belongings" equal belonging. If you think I am bluffing, then I encourage you to think about the Jeep cult subculture so prevalent in the 1990's and 2000's.

I see this trend in myself as well as others: we equate entrance to a group of people when we have the same accoutrements as the group. Picture in your mind someone who is in the process of buying all the trappings of an artist, so she can feel legitimate. She has paints that she has not touched, and is gathering a collection of things that are pricy, and may or may not be used, especially over a long period of time.

Even yours truly falls for the trap. When I was writing books before, I had a 24-inch iMac for composing. "Oh how much more minimal I would be with a laptop," I moaned. As soon as I was debt-free, the iMac got downsized, for a MacBook Air. Do I get more accolades with the laptop? No. But I do get more eye strain with the small screen.

Think about how many of us pay our hard-earned money to be an advertisement for someone else. My house still holds an Abercrombie and Fitch long-sleeved shirt from when we were wanting to belong to the in-crowd.

Think of it, you pay an exorbitant amount to wear a brand of clothing to advertise for someone else. That clothing most likely is flimsily made by the hands of people who will never see the same standard of living as you. Your life will not be magically transported to a fantasy land by wearing the clothing, cooking with the kitchen utensils, or driving the debt-laden car around your neighborhood that you have seen advertised.

But, we all have a deep drive to belong. We all need to fit in, to have our own crowd. The marketers know this and exploit this - magazine after magazine, billboard after billboard.

> More is actually less. And, less is actually more.

The second lie you need to ditch is "More is better." More is not better.

As was said in the introduction, we are not a happy culture in the United States. We have our problems, and one is that we are trying to buy our way into happiness. Next time you are in a friend's home, look at all the stuff. Stuff! Stuff upon stuff! We have our houses chock-full; and we are miserable. We don't realize that having more is not going to make a dent in our unhappiness. In fact, the stress that comes with owning more and more perpetuates our discontent.

You may find this repetitive, and it is! We went over this phenomenon in the sermon. The proof is in our own lives - undeniably before our eyes - we cannot buy happiness.

The third lie you need to debunk is that minimalism equals austerity. Minimalists lead rich, full lives. It is not about what is taken away, it is what has room made for it by vacating clutter.

Your shopping habit may be stealing time from your family and friends. Your debt may hamper your hobby. You may be stuck at home doing things you don't want to do instead of being able to pick up and travel - extendedly, if you wanted.

Simplifying enables you to live better than when you are surrounded by material traps. Frugality, instead of cutting you off from opportunity, opens up doors that are simply not possible with a mountain of debt.

* * *

Now, for the truths to embrace. Once you weed out the lies in your brain about belonging, identity, and what really matters, you need new truths to embrace to replace the old.

The first, and maybe the most important, is this: sometimes (and oftentimes) for something to be possible, it must first be believed to be so. Unless you can conceive of success in a venture, more than likely you won't attempt it.

So many times we talk ourselves out of great adventures, friendships, and achievements because we don't give it (or ourselves) a chance to succeed. "That will never work" becomes our excuse to sit on the bench and not even try to play.

Simplifying is no different. You must first believe that your life can be wonderfully and radically different. You must believe that you can conquer your collection of Precious Moments and macrame and that you can do differently than so many others around you.

If you look at your mountain of belongings and say, "I can never get this place cleaned up," you will be quite right. So say instead, "How can I get this place cleaned up?" And you crack the door open for success to come in to your abode.

If you look at your finances and say, "I will never get out of debt," you will be spot-on. But if you get angry, really truly livid, that you are a slave to your creditors, you can courageously and methodically demolish your debts and live vastly different to those around you, who are still ensnared.

We need to challenge ourselves constantly with the notion that we can live differently than those around us. We really do have the spunk within ourselves to buck the sick notion that we are what we own. When we do, more time, more money, and less stress await us.

Secondly, I want you to say this, and say it loud: "I am not what I own." I am not what I own! Belongings do not equal belonging. They never did. They don't now. And, under no circumstance does that entrapping lie have to define your future.

You can have a brighter and more sublime future than those trapped in consumerism. When you simplify, you have a grand opportunity. That opportunity is to reshape your values so that acquiring is not what gives you a high, but rather producing and achieving.

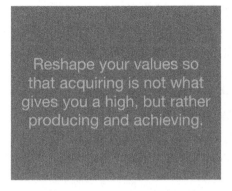

Third, don't remain duped by the culture's messages any longer. Acquiring is not achievement. Acquiring is paying for the privilege of using someone else's achievement. You will not experience the same thrill with acquiring as you will with achieving something of your own.

When you achieve something great (or small) you have a sense of accomplishment. That does not fade easily and it does not go out with the seasons of fashion. You produced. That has merit. No one can take your accomplishment away. You did it. It is yours forever.

When you accomplish your life's goals, you enter a fraternity (or sorority) of a special few who really live well on this planet. Self-actualization is a noble pursuit and touching even the outskirts of it is an enthralling, humbling, and fulfilling experience.

Belongings would like to make you think that you have a brotherhood (or sisterhood) for owning the same thing that a group does, but it is not as cool as achieving, not even close. Acquiring for identity is a cheap imitation of achieving and having identity.

Consuming is not the same as producing. Consuming is playing a video game. Producing is programming and making a video game. It is also the difference between buying wall art, and making your own wall art. You will be more proud of your game that took your sweat and tears and the imperfect but good attempt at a still life painting, than your achievement points and your find at StuffMart.

"Egads! I have fallen for the trap!" you say. That is okay. You are not the first nor the last to have done so. But you don't have to be last for wrestling free of the snare of consumerism either.

Separate your identity from what you own. Make a pact with yourself that you will not define yourself by what you wear, what you drive, or where you live. You are not that simple, anyway.

You are defined by what you think and believe, your actions toward other living beings including family, friends, strangers, and perhaps even plants and animals. Your kindness, or lack thereof, is the most striking piece of adornment you own. You are defined by your relationships with God and others.

What items you own are best viewed as tools. Your clothes are tools to keep you warm and modest.

Your house is a tool to store things in and to sleep in (and indoor plumbing and electricity are awesome). Your car is a tool to transport you, other people, and goods from one place to another. Your food is a tool to give you energy and promote strength for your future endeavors.

There is a wise old joke that goes like this: "How do you eat an elephant?" The answer is, "One bite at a time." There is a lot contained in that joke as far as wisdom on how to approach your Mt. Everest of problem and challenge.

So here is a challenge to you: Believe you are worth a life of sanity and that you can eat the elephant of your obstacles to gain personal growth and serenity. One bite at a time.

We will talk a lot later about the process of eating an elephant made of clutter or debt. For now, I just want you to believe that your dream life is possible, and waiting just beyond the pale when you consider that the socially appropriate lie for you to believe is that "belongings" equal belonging.

Next up is a discourse on benefits of simplifying - just in case you are not yet a believer! Come and learn how getting rid of excess translates into more time, more money, and less stress. You are doing great - keep reading!

# Benefits

What is it that we all want? It is not that simple. There are such differences in people. Some of us want to achieve things. Others want to possess things. More want to be involved in something special. Still others just want to be able to sleep until 11AM in the morning.

But, when you break down how to achieve those things, obtaining what we want usually deals with needing one or more of these three things: more time, more money, or less stress.

Simplifying gives its devotees all three of these benefits in abundance. There is more time, more money, and less stress waiting for you not too far into the journey of simplifying. Those benefits are eager for you to enjoy them, but there are some tradeoffs to get them. (No worries though, what you will trade will likely not be missed much.)

The person who simplifies can get their time back. Time management is part of the path, but there is another component to reclaiming your freedom from unnecessary activities. The component is to reduce your consumption of material goods. The magic of more time begins when you stop shopping.

When you stop shopping, you push a reset button for your life - especially your weekends and evenings. No longer are you

- getting ready

- getting into your vehicle
- traveling to the store
- parking
- going up and down the aisles
- standing in line to check out
- going to your car
- loading your purchases
- driving to the next store
- doing it all over again and again
- driving home
- unpacking
- realizing you have the wrong item
- getting back in your car to return the item(s)

Not-shopping can give you back an afternoon or a precious weekend day (or maybe an entire weekend). In time, it will benefit you a second way - you will spend less time maintaining your stuff, because you have less stuff.

If you simplify, you have an investment up front with creating systems for dealing with your stuff, eliminating the unnecessary, and reshaping habits that got you into the material mess in the first place. But, once that is done, your time can be spent doing other things than cleaning out the garage or attic.

When I first started decluttering, it would take a week, or a week-and-a-half, for me to go through everything in my house and clean out. Over time (and I mean YEARS) the process became easier and easier.

Now, I can go through the contents of my home in the better part of an afternoon; or, if I am super thorough, most of one day is enough for me to corral the unwanted items. Not having surplus makes it quick and easy to assess what is lurking in drawers or on shelves.

My last attack on the garage went especially well. I cleaned and purged the detached one-car building in two hours. And, it got a good going-over and cleaning-out.

You may find that this is your pattern, too. If you put in the investment to get your items under control, you will likely wind up with more time in the not-too-distant future.

Not-shopping and material abstinence also helps provide the second of the three benefits, which is more money.

When we think of money as dollar bills, or as a currency, we have just a small slice of the reality of money. There is something much greater going on during buying and selling, and at the same time, it's more basic. When you understand what really goes on with spending, you may choose to bow out of unnecessary purchases.

Behind all money is an accumulation of power. This is the basic characteristic of money. Money (as an object) is a symbol of that power. A rock can be money, or a paper clip. That paper clip can afford you a penny or a lake house, depending on the value you and someone else assign to that paper clip.

Money in and of itself is worthless. The value must be agreed upon or money doesn't work. Two people at least are required. But once the value is agreed upon the transaction can occur.

Transactions are the transference of power. When you spend money, you are transferring a portion of your personal power to another entity or individual. Let that soak in for a second.

Every time you buy something at StuffMart, you are transferring your power to them. If this makes you sick to think about, good! We are giving power we have, and sometimes power we don't have (when we use credit) to people and corporations that are sometimes fiercely at odds with our own values and beliefs.

 Think about where you want your money to go. Would you trade your power for a cheaply made good that is to impress someone you don't care about? Yet this is what we do, day in, day out when we buy cheap plastic items to fill our homes and when we buy fast fashion flimsies to wear a few times and then discard.

What if you could get to the point where you have enough money to purchase quality items consistently from sellers you want to support and see stay in business? It can happen!

When you simplify and stop shopping for recreation you get more money available…because you haven't spent it! Stopping careless spending and just purchasing your needs and a few wants can really impact your finances in a positive way.

If you are spending less, and spending on things that agree with your value system, what you have will be more meaningful to you. You may find that you value what you own more and it is exactly what you want. You may find that craving to purchase something else abates as well.

The zero waste movement is very important to me. Years ago, I saw a news report on a couple that had a small box of trash that represented everything that would go to a landfill at the end of a year of accumulating. In 2015, I was introduced to Bea Johnson's book, <u>Zero Waste Home</u>. That year, I spent money purchasing things that would help me reduce my waste in the end. It was expensive, but I had the money to do it without stressing our finances.

Now, a little older and a little wiser, I am still able to shop according to my values. I shop at grocery stores where I can get my meat packaged in paper and bulk items in my own Mason jars. I shop package-free as much as possible.

Today I plan to check out a zero waste store in my city. I am super excited, because I have wanted a way to get bulk shampoo and conditioner for years. I experimented with shampoo bars and I am good about recycling my shampoo/conditioner bottles, but have been on the lookout for a better way.

You may find that stopping unnecessary shopping reshapes how you want to spend your money overall. Instead of buying liabilities, you may shift to wanting to acquire assets. Once you break free from the earn-buy-earn cycle, many different possibilities can open up to you.

The earn-buy-earn cycle is a vicious trap for many. They earn money so they can spend money, and then they have to earn more money because they spent the money they had (and a little more) getting the goods and experiences, and there is something sparkly and shiny that they saw last week that is just a little bit out of reach for their bank account now, but come payday it will be within striking distance!

One wintry night a few years ago, I sat down at my dining room table and listed out all the things I had bought - big and small - that came to my mind. After trying to be exhaustive as possible with my inventory, I looked hard at what I had bought in my life.

I estimated then that about 95 percent of what I had bought was liabilities. Those things had decreased or expired in value and I had nothing to show for my purchases. Only about five percent had retained its value or was bringing in money for me still. It was a very sobering realization.

As much as possible, try to buy things that are assets - or things that have the potential to make you more money. Steer clear of excessive liabilities like books, gadgets, and clothes. Start trying to buy things like mutual funds and CDs (certificates of deposit) instead.

So, now we are left with the last benefit of simplifying: less stress. Simplifying promotes less stress because all those annoying piles in our house - bills, laundry, broken-and-needs-fixing items - have been dealt with and are no longer haunting the better part of weekends and evenings.

A simplified home is very often a serene home. Visually, it isn't overwhelming. It is easy to clean and things have a designated place or a "home" within the home. There isn't the hunting for the dealy-bob, because you know where it and its purple sister reside in your house.

You may start to feel less stress with one thorough purge of your dwelling. Just doing away with the excess - as it is defined in your own mind - allows you to rest easy.

The less stress will take root and grow with subsequent purges as you are ready for them. As you set up systems for dealing with the stuff in your home you gain a sense of control over your belongings.

One of the defining characteristics of a minimalist is that they do not procrastinate. Their level of delaying and letting things slide is very slight compared to a normal person.

This attention to things and responsibilities is a cultivated habit. It does not come naturally. It is a trait that is groomed and fertilized in the life of a minimalist, and it pays off hugely for the person who adopts it.

When something comes up on the radar of a minimalist - like an unpaid bill, or the need for a doctor's appointment - instead of throwing the statement aside or shrugging off that pulsing tooth, a check is written and a stamp is put on the envelope that day or evening. The dentist is called, or a note to call first thing in the morning is made and put in a prominent place.

Further, calendars are marked with dates reserved to purge the house or dwelling. Laundry is folded. Family members have chores delegated to them and are expected to pitch in to help with the maintenance of the home.

Not letting your house go into shambles is a huge morale booster. Maybe you don't have a day that you can devote to cleaning. Try doing a few things toward house spiffing every night, When the dishes need doing, it will always be in the back of your mind. When they are done, it is relaxing to your brain, and you can better relax on your couch for the rest of the evening.

Simplifying your finances also promotes having less stress. You have confidence that you can pay the light bill and go out to dinner with your friends on Thursday. Financial responsibility does not come naturally to most of us, but it is well worth cultivating. It is absolutely amazing what a slush fund of savings can do to decrease your stress level.

Getting out of debt is so huge! It is truly a game-changer. Retiring all debt will result in what will likely be the biggest pay raise you ever get in your entire life. Not convinced? If your house payment is $700 per month, and you blast your mortgage to kingdom-come, suddenly you just increased your spending power by $700 per month. Bet your employer is unlikely ever to do the same favor for you!

Simplifying your time and practicing time management will allow you to not be stressed to the gills. It is possible to control most of your free time and do activities that bring you satisfaction and that feel rewarding. Much will be said later about time management and simplifying. For now, just know that it is possible.

So now we are to the Day of Reconciliation. This is where you start finding the coordinates of your financial map. To know where you want to go, you must first know where you are and then be able to gauge the distance of how to get there.

The Day of Reconciliation is your starting point. I am not going to lie, it can be scary to see the numbers. But, you need to face it. You need to know the truth about your financial situation. The fear can be a catalyst for change.

Read through the next section thoroughly before attempting it. This takes some prior planning and setting some time aside, but it is so important! Go ahead, get your bearings. You will be ready to dive into the simplification lifestyle shortly!

# Day of Reconciliation

The following was ripped out of my first book, <u>Minimize: Kill your debt. Live your dream.</u>, that I wrote in late 2013. It was written well enough the first time, so it bears repeating.

* * *

Another preparation for getting radical on your debt is a Day of Reconciliation. I highly recommend making this important and pressing on your calendar, and make it an event for you, and (hopefully) an adult with whom you share finances, if you have one.

Mark off an entire day (or more, if you think you will need it) for the Day of Reconciliation. Protect this time on your calendar. Ask off from work if you need it. Your financial health is worth a vacation day!

It is optional if you want to get dressed on this day. Jammies are fine attire. Fix a simple breakfast (something quick without much clean up) and then begin.

Round up all your financial documents. The latest bank statements. The latest 401k statements. Stocks count as well. Paycheck stubs, too. Also, find credit card statements for every card you own. Find statements on anything "rent to own," and, of course, your latest mortgage and car loan statement. If something comes to mind that is not listed here, get it!

Get a calculator and some blank paper and a pen. List all of your assets (the equity in your home, stocks that are turning a profit, 401k and IRAs, savings accounts, checking account balances, everything) on one side of the paper. If there is not room for everything, start another page.

Next, list your liabilities. List credit card balances, loan balances, rent-to-own balances, etc. List everything!

Now, add up each column. Then compare the two totals. This is your net worth. On paper, this is what you are worth to the world, but this is not your true worth. Is the number negative? That's okay. You now know the extent of the problem.

|   | Asset | Value | Debt | Amount owed |
|---|-------|-------|------|-------------|
| 1 | 401k | 23,369 | Car 1 | 6,598 |
| 2 | Stocks | 4,568 | Car 2 | 8,975 |
| 3 | Savings | 1,569 | House | 58,798 |
| 4 |  |  | Washer/dryer | 697 |
| 5 |  |  | Credit card 1 | 4,982 |
| 6 |  |  | Credit card 2 | 2,934 |
| 7 |  |  |  |  |

|  | Asset | Value | Debt | Amount owed |
|---|---|---|---|---|
| 8 | | | | |
| Total | | 29,506 | | -82,984 |
| Difference | -53,478 | | | |

You might break for lunch now if you haven't already. Don't leave the house for lunch; you might break the momentum. Get a pizza ordered in; or, prepare for this day in advance so you will be ready.

Was lunch good? Good! Now we are ready for part two: your earning potential.

Now, what I want you to do is list every source of income you have during a month. This is your paycheck, interest on savings accounts, dividends from stocks; everything that is regular and that contributes to your income goes in a column.

Now make a column for your bills. Credit card bills, average utility bills, phone bills, internet bills, gym memberships, insurance, cable, everything that costs you money (like average grocery bills). We will get to eating out in a moment.

Okay. Add the two and find the difference between your cash flow and your outgo. Are you scared now? Pleasantly surprised? Horrified? At least, now you know. Here, knowing truly is "half the battle."

| | Item | Amount | Item | Amount |
|---|---|---|---|---|
| | Visa | 40 | Paycheck 1 | 1500 |
| | Car | 300 | Babysitting | 40 |
| | House | 750 | Paycheck 2 | 800 |
| | Gym | 20 | | |
| | Groceries | 500 | | |
| | Insurance | 200 | | |
| | | | | |
| | | | | |
| Total | | 1810 | | 2340 |
| Difference | +530 | | | |

If there is a positive difference between your bills and your income, that is considered your discretionary income. That is money that can be used for eating out and other treats. Use that money to pay down your debts instead. What you don't spend on sushi or hamburgers you can use to pay down your credit cards.

Since you are here, please make a list of all your debts. I do mean everything. Try to list them from smallest to largest, and include the interest rate on the figures on the paper so that everything is handy.

You may also like to add in the minimum payment due. This will help you decide what to pay on first. Dave Ramsey recommends doing this exercise and I will touch more on what his book, The Total Money Makeover, says a little later.

|  | Debt | Amount | Interest Rate (%) |
|---|---|---|---|
| 1 | Washing Machine | 139 | 11 |
| 2 | Credit Card 3 | 236 | 18 |
| 3 | Title loan | 469 | 22 |
| 4 | Car 1 | 968 | 7 |
| 5 | Credit card 2 | 1,569 | 19 |
| 6 | Car 2 | 7,906 | 7.5 |
| 7 | Credit Card 3 | 9,521 | 14 |
| 8 | Student Loans | 49,563 | 10 |
| 9 |  |  |  |
| 10 |  |  |  |

Are you done with your reconciliation? Good! Have a small treat - go for a long walk, pet the dog, cat, or goldfish (if the fish will let you). You have made a truly great start in rectifying your situation.

Now you know where you stand. You have your net worth, a picture of your monthly intake and outgo. You also know the extent of your debts.

The debt snowball is a concept worth mentioning here. It is a staple in Dave Ramsey's teachings (and I think he is very much worth a look if you are swimming in debt).

The idea of the debt snowball is to pay your smallest debt first, and keep everything else current. Then when the first debt is paid, the money that went toward that payment is added to the next smallest debt and applied until the second smallest debt is retired. Then the money from the first and second debt goes toward the next largest debt until that is retired, and so on, until all the debt has been paid except for the house.

Let me be clear - I did not follow Dave Ramsey's plans to get my finances under control. My life has revolved around staying as debt-free as possible. The only debt we carried in our marriage apart from the HVAC purchase was our house. We had our cars paid off when we came to the marriage, and we have not gone into debt for education or anything since then - and we have both been through college while married.

But, when I discovered Mr. Ramsey's teachings, I could find no beef with them. They are sound, and they do work, and I highly recommend his strategy for conquering debt and getting in the black.

So, listen to me, and listen to Dave. If you are in debt, use the steps Ramsey outlines in his books to conquer it. If you can, stay out of debt as much as possible, even for major purchases. If you have to take on debt, treat it like your hair is on fire (I got that visual from Mr. Money Mustache - a wonderful blogger that retired when he was 30).

The point at which I deviate from Dave Ramsey is when he talks about getting the toys without debt. I invite you to do without the toys completely, and live a wonderful life without a lot of stuff.

This manual will focus mainly on decluttering and frugality. For a strategy about getting out of debt, take time to read <u>The Total Money Makeover</u>, or check for Financial Peace University courses in your area (also a Dave Ramsey item).

Be assured, he did not pay me to tell you this. This recommendation comes from my heart to you. There is no need to re-invent the wheel. He nailed it on sound strategy to get control of your finances.

Now, let's start talking about what to do with your knickknack collection and Star Wars figurines. Next up: intro to decluttering. (We're HERE!)

# Introduction to Decluttering

The first order of business is to make a clear distinction between decluttering and organizing. One is far superior to the other, in my opinion, and they should be done in a specific order.

First, and most important, is decluttering. This is where items you no longer want and need leave your possession. This is what should be done first during a purge.

Organizing is the lesser. Why? Because you are shuffling your stuff around and storing it in a rubber tote at the back of your closet. You still have the responsibility of care and maintenance of it, and you are not yet free of it.

Declutter over organize is the way to go. When you are done with a round of decluttering and purging, then organize what is left. Try to use what you have instead of buying fancy and costly containers. Velveeta cheese boxes make great drawer dividers, for instance, and there are plenty DIY (do it yourself) hacks out there that can take common items and fit a need.

Thrifty is the way to go, and the words of eight years of wisdom, because the deeper you go into simplifying, less organizers will be needed. You likely may purchase items to help organize, only to have the tote and the contents do a march out your door in six months to a few years' time.

If you believe that you will declutter once and be done, you will be disappointed. Decluttering is a journey, not a destination. Your

> **Food for Thought:**
>
> Conserve your resources and think cheap, especially in the beginning.

belongings are in a constant state of flux. You generate trash in your home daily, and you bring in items to be used, and eventually disposed of, on a regular basis.

But the good news is that decluttering leads to a state for your stuff that is a snap to maintain. This is called "The Essential," and it is your perfect level of ownership of material goods. You have something wonderful to look forward to if you declutter.

At The Essential, you have what you need and a few wants. Everything you own is either useful or beautiful to you. There is order, and your possessions have designated "homes" within your dwelling. You can find things easily and you know off the top of your head where almost everything you own is lurking. There are systems set up in your home for dealing with incoming stuff, as well as systems for responsibly disposing of no longer needed items.

The Essential is where it is as though your stuff breathes. When something comes in, something else goes out. When something goes out, something comes in to your space. The level of

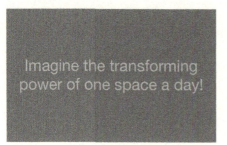

stuff never changes greatly. It is like homeostasis in a sense. It is almost magical.

Yes, there will be swelling occasionally, but with minimal effort, the swelling or influx of stuff will be deflated down to its normal amount. When you declutter (and you will still declutter at The Essential) you will find that beyond a small amount, there is really nothing to part with in your home.

You don't have to guess whether you are at The Essential. You will know it when you are there! The arrangement of stuff will make sense to you. You will feel complete and like there is nothing lacking. You will have peace with your possessions.

Start small. This concept was first introduced to me through Francine Jay, also known as Miss Minimalist. She said to start with one thing per day. So, start with a drawer or a shelf. If you have only 15 minutes a day to devote to decluttering, devote 15 minutes. Don't give up on the idea due to a lack of time.

If you declutter one drawer a day, at the end of the month that could be as much as 31 spaces downsized and organized. At the end of the year it would be over 300 spaces in your home that have been decluttered.

When you are decluttering to start your journey, you may find yourself filling up half of a room with cast-offs. Don't worry though, that is not the way it will be forever. With time, the piles will get smaller and smaller, and the time spent decluttering will be less and less intensive.

When starting, decluttering your house methodically can take a week or more. You may need to do it again shortly after completing a major clean-out (and by, "shortly," I mean a few months, not hours). But, you will start to see a change. What took you a week to clean out a year ago may take you a few days this year. After more time, what took you a few days may take you only a day.

The Essential for me came in April of 2015, after I had what I hope is the last garage sale of my life. The furniture has stayed about the same. We are preparing to trade our futon for a chaise sleeper sofa and our leather chair for a chair to match the sofa. The negative space vs occupied space has remained about the same. The decor has changed somewhat, but there hasn't been a surge or exodus of knickknacks and framed deco art.

My clothing has gotten overhauled a few times, but the amount of clothes has roughly remained constant. We have not needed to buy a great deal of things for new storage.

The Essential is worth the trouble. My simplified house doesn't stress me. My friends compliment me on how peaceful and serene it seems. It definitely is not due to posh decorating - we are on a budget, by golly! But, it is a cinch to clean and almost effortless to maintain.

And, it is quite possible, and has been done before, that you can successfully declutter a house, 1100 square feet in size, in the better part of an afternoon and clean it in about an hour-and-a-half…if you are at The Essential.

# How to Eat an Elephant: Purging

There are several different schools of thought about undertaking the decluttering process, or purging. Some say to go in categories, piling up all clothes, books, etc., and going through everything at once. Some say to go quickly, making decisions based on feeling.

Remember the joke that was mentioned: How do you eat an elephant? The answer is "one bite at a time." A seemingly impossible feat is accomplished in a plethora of baby steps. I am going to show you how you can eat your elephant of clutter.

One bite at a time is the approach that can tackle a mountain of clutter without feeling overwhelmed or burned-out. This is when you know that you are in the decluttering game for the long-haul, and you view paring down your possessions as a marathon and not a 40-yard dash.

It is not uncommon for decluttering to take months or years. It took five years to reach The Essential after I started purging in late 2009 or early 2010. The reason for this lies within the truth that our piles of clutter usually took years to create, and they will take a length of time to undo.

Also, clutter is like an onion. You peel a layer back and you see a new layer underneath. You peel the second layer back, and, behold! There is a third layer smiling up at you from under the second.

You may think you have successfully decluttered everything in your home and time will pass. Maybe a few days or a few months pass and then you start noticing things that you didn't get rid of, but could… couldn't you? Decluttering is truly a journey and not a destination. You continually arrive, and yet you are never completely finished.

When you embrace this truth, you are ready to be happy with the process of eliminating the waste and finding homes for your no longer wanted treasures. Decluttering can become a natural act, and living with less can be a desirable way to live, as has been discovered by many on the simplification journey.

I do want to take a moment to tell you that if you are not ready to purge, that is okay. You need to take this process at your own pace and in your own time for the best results. There have been times I gave up things too quickly and had regrets. I don't want that for you. Go as slowly as you need to, but realize it is fine to go quickly if you know you are ready to let go of a lot.

So, are you ready for eating some elephant? Start small. Do one drawer, or one shelf at a time. Don't focus on the overall picture, or even a room at a time. One drawer. One shelf. One surface.

As was said in the introduction to decluttering, our small, daily accomplishments will add up over time. If you were to do a drawer per day, that is potentially

31 drawers in a month! If you were to declutter a surface a day for a year, that is 365 surfaces cleaned and decluttered - without killing yourself trying to get there.

There are several methods out there for the actual process of decluttering. The method that you use is up to you, but I believe it should have some elements of the following:

Clear the Surface

Take the time to take everything out of the drawer or container or off the surface or shelf. Everything. This means the salt shaker gets off the table, the shoes journey away from their place in the closet, the canisters are removed from the cabinet. Everything.

Make Piles

Move quickly and make a pile (the exception to this is fragile objects which may need to have their own space) of all the items you just removed from your surfaces. It doesn't have to make sense at this point, it just has to be in one central location.

Sort the Piles

Now, you are going to get down to serious business! You can make labels with a piece of paper and marker and lay the paper spread out on the floor.

You can use boxes. You can skip the labels. But, now you are going to make meaningful piles of stuff.

Use categories that make sense to you. When first starting out, separate categories really come in handy to help designate what the stuff needs to do next. The categories that are favorites are: Keep, Donate, Sell, Mend, Trash, I-Have-No-Clue.

Start taking items from the main pile and separate them into what they logically go in as far as subcategories are concerned. For things you want to donate to charity or someone else, put them in "Donate." For things you want to sell: "Sell." Mending is for things that you can and will actually fix and use again. If you have no idea where to start diagnosing your burned-up microwave, see if you can recycle it, or just let it go along to "Trash."

I-Have-No-Clue is where things go that you don't know if you can let go of yet, but you know you don't need it immediately. A box or tote in the garage or closet is a great place for Just-In-Case items with which you are having difficulty parting. Put all the things in this pile in a box, close it up, and store it for six months. You may even want to put the date you boxed it up or the date you want to revisit the contents on the outside of the box. If you can't tell yourself what is in the box at the end of the time, go ahead and let it go, preferably without looking inside the box again.

Clean the Surface

Really give the surface a good scrub. Get all the cobwebs off, all the dirt out, and make it sparkle as best you can. This will help you connect to your belongings and dwelling on a deeper level. It is also good to maintain what you own.

Put the Keep Back

Now you can put the items in "Keep" back on your newly decluttered and spiffed surface or storage container. Try to make the arrangement meaningful and logical. If you have items in your "Keep" pile that belong in another place in your home, go take care of the transition at this point in the process!

Make the Space Sacred

Claiming the space after you have it mastered is a crucial part of continued success. Don't let clutter roost in your sacred space! When something lands on the surface, take care of it promptly. Do not delay! This practice will save you repeating and repeating the same decluttering song and dance over and over, year after year.

Practice a "Clutter Blitz" daily. You can set a timer if you like, but the idea is to spend about 15 minutes just rounding up clutter in your home and putting it back where it belongs before it takes up residence where you don't want it. This small practice will save you many headaches down the road.

Also, try early on in your purging to form the habit of 1 in/3 out. That is, for every one item you bring in, three like items leave your home. One book in, three books out. One shirt in, three shirts out.

As you get to where you want to be with your level of stuff, you can choose to form a 1 in/1 out rule. For every item you bring in, an item leaves your home.

We are preparing to switch out our living room furniture, and we are trading a futon for a sofa, and a chair for a chair. We are also swapping a desk and a coffee table for two ottomans. We are adding a rug, but our old rug went away years ago when our beloved Siamese had a thing about relieving herself on carpet. (That may be more information than you needed.)

Get Rid of the Cast Offs

The final step of decluttering is to offload the cast-away items. This can be a daunting task; but it is oh, so necessary, and rewarding, when it is done expediently and efficiently.

As much as possible, try to keep your rejects from going in a landfill. There is enough trash on the planet as it is. Recycle what you can, re-gift what you cannot. For the items that cannot do either of those, the dump might have to do.

Search out recycling centers in your city or town. It may surprise you what can be salvaged. There is a recycling center in my city that will take anything with a cord or a battery. There are also places that will accept light bulbs and shred documents; and, there are some services that will take hazardous waste, like paint, for a fee. You just need to know where to look. Call your local government and ask about available recycling centers in your area.

If you have items to donate, give them to charity quickly before you change your mind. Old clothes need not go to a landfill unless they are beyond repair. Slightly out of date can be someone's go-to item still. Furniture, kitchenware, books, DVDs, and more can be someone's treasure after you are done with them. Search for available charities online. Some drop-off locations may be near you, and some charities offer pick-up of items. That is especially handy for getting rid of items that didn't sell after a garage sale.

If you have items for other people, get them to their intended owners as soon as possible. You can even mail the item, if it is not possible to easily or quickly get the loot to your loved one. Call and set up a time to get the items to their new owners. You will likely be so glad you did.

For items you want to sell, think about where you might have a buyer. Pawn shops are not off limits for sure. Jewelry can be sold to a jeweler for scrap in my city. Craigslist is good for certain items,

Facebook has a marketplace set up in some cases for items to be sold or traded. eBay is another option. If you have a message board at your work or local business, that may be another choice.

For things that you are not sure of where to offload, try to go "up the food chain." What I mean by this is, ask those who sell the items you are trying to offload what they do with their castoffs. The most exciting example that I have of this is when I changed my own windshield wipers.

I was barely done congratulating myself on figuring out how to swap the wipers out on my car when I realized that now I had two very ungainly pieces of trash. I didn't put them in my garbage right away.

I went up the food chain and took myself and the wipers to my mechanic's shop. I asked at the desk if they knew how to recycle the wipers. It just so happened that there was a worker in the shop that turned wipers into artwork on the side. Win-win. My wipers didn't go in the trash and stayed out of the landfill. An artist got free supplies; and I walked away empty-handed and happy.

When you are thinking about selling, you must know your comfort level with what price you are willing to accept, and what is too low for you. Just be aware that because you are not willing to accept a few dollars less, that clunky, cumbersome item is going to squat another night in your possession because you wouldn't come down on your price. But if price is important, and more important than offloading, then you need to stick to your insistence on the price you have chosen.

More is to come on what to do with castoff items. Stay tuned and turn the page. Eight-and-a-half years of hard-won advice is coming your way!

# Offloading Stuff

You are going to tell me at some point that offloading all excess stuff sounds amazing in theory, but you paid good money for that dinglewhazit and you can't just let it go.

Here are some creative ways I have used to try to offload stuff:

eBay

My mom had some Willow figurines that we couldn't figure out how to discard. I suggested eBay to her and she was interested, provided I do all the dirty work for her.

We took pictures of the group of figurines (because we were selling as a group to get rid of everything at once). I figured out how to post them on eBay and we waited.

We had someone buy them fairly quickly. I then had to figure out how to ship the figurines to the buyer and then waited to collect her money. It went to PayPal after the buyer released it and all was well.

Sometimes it is not as successful. My husband and I were in possession of a nice watch that retailed at about $130 for some company kickback gift of some sort for one of us. (I don't even remember the gory details now of how we came to have that in our possession; can you tell?) We listed it on eBay. No takers. Not even one iota of interest. We wound up giving the watch to a family member to try to sell who needed some quick cash.

So, sometimes it works, sometimes it doesn't. Same with Craigslist.

Amazon

I have not sold much on Amazon, but they are worth mentioning for one specific group of troublesome items I had: textbooks. I went through the trade-in process on several of my old PTA textbooks from my schooling. I didn't get a fortune for them, but for some I was offered 30 dollars or more; and I didn't have to pay to ship them to Amazon. I received Amazon credit for my trade-ins; and I had no trouble figuring out how to spend my allowance. No trouble at all.

Message Boards

There is a message board in the cafeteria where I work. I have used that on occasion to offload bikes that were unwanted. Look for message boards in the community. Coffee shops are sometimes good places to post. Cafeterias are another. Just check with the manager or owner of the business before you put a thumbtack in their wall.

Jewelry Stores

I had some gold jewelry that I didn't want anymore. I chose to go to a local jewelry store that bought scrap gold. I received over $100.00 for a few pieces on a couple of occasions, and was no longer burdened with storing unwanted baubles.

Used Book Stores - ABC Books

In my city there is a wonderful used book store that is fabulous about taking trade-ins. When I was whittling down my paperback collection I would visit them with a stack, and leave with one or two special books that I wanted to read. Sometimes it would be six or seven books leaving and one coming in. When you are minimizing, that sounds like a good trade, and the books didn't go in the trash!

Used Clothing Stores - Clothes Mentor

Clothes Mentor was my go-to place to sell and buy clothes for a short, but special, season of my life. I would pick up name brands at a fraction of the cost for them new. They were still relevant, and I still wear pieces I got there with pride, even though the store has been gone for about a year.

I also sold clothes to them, sometimes they were pieces I bought there! I didn't get outstanding prices for the items most times, but I got more out of them at Clothes Mentor than I would have at a garage sale.

Alltec

There is a wonderful computer center in Missouri called Alltec. They will buy, sell, and repair computers of almost any make or model. I bought my first Mac there, and sold that same iMac back to them three years later when I was upgrading to a laptop.

I also recycled a laptop with them. They allowed me to take my hard drive out and destroy it the way I wanted. I don't remember if there was a fee to do the recycling with them; but, it was a pleasant experience, and the laptop didn't go to the dump.

Speaking of recycling: for things that you know you can part with, without getting money for them, think of recycling before the dump. I have had good success with getting rid of things that might be deemed troublesome through the years. Here are some items, avenues, and companies for getting rid of recyclables

Automobiles and Parts

It was a happy surprise when our Cavalier was totaled that we did not have to pay the salvage yard to tow our ill-fated mechanical family member to its grave. They paid us. It was a simple process. I called the salvage company, they came and assessed the car, made their offer, took the title, and hauled it off.

Electronics

More on the Computer Recycling Center in my city that is such a resource: Not only do they boast they will take anything with a cord or a battery, I have offloaded coffee makers, old TVs (the boxy kind), lamps that were suspect for becoming fire hazards, radios, and more. See if there is something similar in your area. Some cities have lists of where you can get everything that can be recycled, disposed of, in that city.

1-800-GOT-JUNK

I have used 1-800-GOT-JUNK three times and have been happy all three times. These people take everything I set out, no questions asked. I have given items that are hard to dispose of to them and I find their fees are reasonable. In my experience they are extremely professional, efficient, and quick. When they leave my driveway, I feel a great burden lifted from my shoulders.

Clothing Beyond Repair

I have heard the advice given, and I have given it myself and taken it into consideration, that old clothes that cannot be donated or sold can be made into cleaning rags. But, let's face it. You only need so many rags! Some charities will have the option for you to bag up your clothes that cannot be given new life and donate them as rags. The charities have avenues where they will grind up the unusable clothes to be recycled into other things.

If you choose to do this, contact the charity of your choice first and see if this is an option. For some it is, others not. Be courteous and don't dump. If you can donate, make sure you clearly mark the box or bag as rags to save some poor worker time from sorting out your clothes.

Sweet'n Low Packages

Why do I mention this? Because you can cut your trash down by recycling as much as you can. My family is on bag trash service, so we pay for every bag we use. It makes sense to put out as little as possible. So for sweetener packages, we recycle those with our paper. Same with post-it notes. Nothing is too small to not go in the recycling bin, if it can be recycled.

As a result of our retentive ways, we have saved a bundle on trash service through the last several years. Were we on a cart service, we would spend more for sure. With the bags, our average cost yearly for trash pick-up is between $50-$70.

Cartridge World

I occasionally have papers that are too much in volume for my shredder and my patience, so I take the stack to Cartridge World and pay by the pound (and it is reasonable) to have my papers put in a locked bin and then properly shredded by the company. I have never had a problem with doing this. Once I took them 26 pounds of paper at one time.  Never again.  That was before I quit procrastinating.

Pet Supplies

Cali, our Siamese kitty, went on hospice earlier this year and has since passed.  When we were sure that we would no longer need certain meds, we took the excess back to our vet.  (And, due to my stock-up attitude toward having her prescription food, anti-nausea med, and probiotics on hand, we had quite a supply.)

We use Angel Animal Hospital for our pet care services and were thrilled when they offered to buy back our unused medications that had been issued by their office.  We donated pill pockets to be used with a low-income family with a beloved kitty.  Very little could not be reclaimed out of what we had accumulated with Cali's care.

By now, you may see a trend.  Go up the food chain whenever possible for items that don't readily appear to be able to be reused or recycled.  Think creatively when trying to sell things.

Don't underestimate the power of a good garage sale, but keep in mind if you need a higher value out of something, a yard sale won't give you much return on investment, because people are looking for supremo bargains at those things.

Again, try to keep as much as possible out of the waste stream. Our landfills have been given enough love through the years of American consumption.

Now we will cover some tools for decluttering and making the progress last and last. We will cover attitudes and habits that will keep money in your wallet and a smile on your heart. Now that we have talked about the exterior, let's talk about the interior, or time management.

Curious? Excited? Turn the page! It's time to start downsizing your calendar and obligations.

# Time Management

There are a few habits that I find very, very helpful in managing my time. Single-focus goal setting is one, and making lists is another. Also, batching things takes the repetitive sting out of drudgery tasks like cooking and errand running.

Single-focus goal setting involves attending to your most important task first and foremost. There is a quote I appreciate greatly about attending to the most glaring thing early on in your day that has been attributed to Mark Twain and also a Frenchman of the 18th century. It doesn't really matter who said it, because it is poignant nevertheless.

Rephrased: do your most important task first thing.

If you don't choose to eat your biggest frog first, you will have that slimy amphibian on the back of your mind until you do. It will be a nagging distraction to the rest of what you attempt.

> "If it's your job to eat a frog, it's best to do it first thing in the morning. And If it's your job to eat two frogs, it's best to eat the biggest one first."
>
> -Mark Twain (?)

Making your day's priorities with the biggest one first will help you focus in on what really needs your attentions. To-do lists are great, and I use them daily. I build my daily list around one, or maybe two things, that are outstandingly, unquestionably more important than everything else.

CJ, my awesome hubby, does the same thing with his days off from his job. When we have coffee together on our coinciding free days, I will ask him "So, what are your plans today?" He will reply almost without fail, "Work on my game and go to the gym."

That is what is most important to him, and that is what he makes time for when he has the choice. He does other things that are around those two things, such as helping me with house work, running errands for me or with me, or going over to a friend's house for a guys-only barbecue and Walking Dead episode.

By not having a list of 10 or more things to do, we ensure that what is truly important to us will get done unless an act of God occurs. We know our priorities and we act accordingly.

And, if you think about it, it makes sense to do the most important task first. That way, you have the whole day to devote to it, if necessary. You may stand a greater chance of getting what you want done, done, if you have more than a few hours of daylight to devote to your project.

The benefits of single-focus goal setting are enormous. Most days I do not feel defeated by time and chance. I have done what I have set out to do;

and I do not feel overwhelmed. So, go ahead. Eat that frog!

The second practice I have that really helps me stay on track is making lists. List-making may seem counterintuitive because of the time spent making lists. Trust me, though, this practice's payoffs are huge.

I make different kinds of lists. I list what I want in my ideal life. I list what I want to do that day. I list where I wanted to purge, room by room. I list what I want to accomplish before and after work on my weekends that I labor. I list my shopping for groceries. And, if you don't think yet that I am retentive, know this: I also make a list of clothing items I want when I shop for my spring/summer and fall/winter wardrobes.

I list what I want to deep-clean room by room. (That set of lists I keep in my computer so I can print out a copy when I am ready for my deep cleaning expedition. The way I clean doesn't change much from year to year, so I keep a master list in my files and tweak as necessary. It is also uplifting to have a printed list to follow.) If it can be a list, I make a list.

I had a desk in my living room which was command center for all of this. That desk was where I kept my day planner, my sheets of paper for planning daily stuff, my grocery lists (I added to them throughout the week), and what I needed to remember to bring with me when I went to my parents' homes or to a friend's house.

I keep a week-at-a-glance planner going throughout the year. Every appointment goes into this planner. Also, every social event goes into this planner. I write down the dates I work; and, if I have a project I want to accomplish, like painting pallets with my mom or cleaning the gutters with CJ, that goes in the planner also.

Once a week or so, I sit down and map out the week ahead from my planner to six separate sheets of paper (the weekend shares a sheet). When I do this, I try to start mapping out my day with morning activities at the top and evening activities at the bottom. Then, as I go through the day on the day I rip the sheet of paper starting at the top and just focus on my morning tasks. In the afternoon I may rip the paper again to just have my afternoon tasks glaring at me. At the end of the day I am usually left with a small piece of paper and a manageable amount of stuff left to do.

CJ makes fun of me for using paper in the Digital Age. But, it is the system that makes the most sense to me. You may like to use your phone or computer, and that is fine. Just do what works for you.

In my defense, I do use the notes feature of my Mac products to make impromptu notes to myself, especially when I am at work or too lazy to walk across the room to write it down. Because my phone and Mac talk to each other, I can easily access my notes later to…write it down on my planner or paper!

A habit that I have that I don't know of anyone else in my circle doing is, to take a blank sheet of paper and pen, sit down, pray, and, then start writing the things that come to mind as far as tasks are concerned. This habit keeps me on top of things very effectively. I will write both short- and long-range tasks. Some things that have come to mind before are to make doctors' appointments, schedule time with friends, or do chores around the house.

I make the list until I feel empty inside. This may be a 30-minute or more endeavor, but it pays off hugely. Hardly anything slips through the cracks. I don't usually have the event of remembering things and forgetting things, only to remember them again when it is too late. My system makes me very effective at staying up on business things related to running a house and being a functioning member of society.

Another thing you can do to make the most of your limited time is to batch things. Examples of this are errand running and cooking.

If you keep a list of non-critical errands that you need to run; and then, when you have a chunk of time, run those errands in one grand trip, you will feel efficient; and my bet is you will be efficient.

Plan your route so that you back-track as little as possible. You can even plan your route to make as many right-hand turns as opposed to left-hand turns as possible, because left-hand turns are more costly as far as time goes.

Batching cooking is a huge time saver for busy families. The idea is to prep and make as much as you can for the week ahead at one time, so you just pull it out of the fridge or freezer and heat as necessary.

I have experimented with this on a small and large scale. In January, 2017, I made 20 bag-dinners that took up my entire freezer and slowly over the next few months when I needed a dinner I took a bag out, thawed it overnight, popped it in the slow cooker the next day, and had a hot meal waiting for me in the evening. This was fairly successful.

Lately, I try to make lunches for the weekend when I work, and make sure my husband has something he can pull and heat up, too. A big pot of soup and bread has been a fantastic way to prep for lunches when I am working. I have also been cutting up chicken and cooking it ahead to put in sauces like Tikka Masala, Marinara, or Alfredo to be served with rice or pasta for an easy evening meal. I also make big pans of meatballs and then stick them in a mason jar in the fridge. When I need a quick pasta dish during the week, I pull a few meatballs, heat them, and voila! Dinner is a hit!

It is a big time-sink up front. I plan to spend most of my Friday afternoon today cooking chicken and making salsa, zucchini soup, and lentil soup. But in the days to come I will save myself a little agony over what is for dinner.

There is only one major cleanup, also.

> **Take Action:**
>
> List everything you know you need to do on a sheet of paper. Look over the list. Choose what is the most important thing you need to do. Do that thing and mark it off your list.

Take to heart the five P's. (Prior planning prevents poor performance.) The more you plan for things, the better off you will be, in my opinion. You will be more effective, efficient, and in the end, less stressed. Stay focused. Write down your tasks in a central location. Batch things whenever possible. Stick to your lists as much as possible.

You may now think that we are done with lists, but no! We have some budgeting to do. Listing out expenses with your finances is an important first step toward financial healing. The self-education that comes with knowing the truth about your finances is ginormous; and, it allows you to make intelligent choices.

You've got this! Keep going - you are on a great track!

# The Lazy Budget

To me, the biggest advantage of budgeting is the self-education that comes with knowing the truth about my financial picture. In presentations that I made at a Health System during 2017-2018, I had some poignant stories about how the truth is able to set you free.

The first story I told was about my and my husband's nasty little Starbucks habit back in the early 2000's. My husband and I worked at a callcenter for a local communications company. There was a grocery store with a Starbucks kiosk inside and we would swing by every morning and get a drink and something to eat for each of us.

I tracked this for a month. Guess how much we were spending on breakfast. Two hundred dollars you say? Try $360. On breakfast!

Another wart on my reputation as a frugal person was my mocha habit at my workplace. The hospital had a coffee shop on the ground floor. Every morning I would get a coffee drink, and every afternoon I would get a smoothie (none of this was reduced-fat, by the way).

I persevered in this wayward behavior until a coworker who was a COTA at the time said with a slight drawl, "Ya know, for what you spend on that afternoon smoothie, you could have a $700 bike in a year's time."

I sneered at him. I called him a liar and then on second thought got out a calculator. I nearly had to change my shorts when I hit the sum button. I indeed could have a $700 bike in a year's time if I cut out just the afternoon smoothie. Just the smoothie!

So, I happily confess, a year later I was riding around on Gretel, my shiny new city bike. And, I was a few pounds lighter.

It isn't just my experience with this sort of thing. The first person I helped with my ministry was eager to learn my style of budgeting; and so we sat down month-after-month, for five months; and then rigged the math to give her a year's outlook on her finances.

There was a very dramatic pause at my kitchen table. Then she quietly said, "For what I am spending on facials and massages, I could take a Caribbean vacation almost every year." And it was true, she could have.

But, she would never have known that without the math. And, I would probably still be getting breakfast at Starbucks if I hadn't done the math.

The budget method I have used for the last five years can be done on two sheets of paper. You will need a calculator and a pen or a pencil. It is so simple, and effective. I call it the Lazy Budget.

The first thing to do before starting your budget is to track expenses for a month. I mean everything. Write down to the penny what you spend and what you earn. Packs of gum count as expenses. A nickel found in a parking lot counts as income. Nothing is too small to escape your notice.

When I say to the penny, I mean to the penny. Don't round off numbers unless you absolutely must. If you know it was $12.34, put $12.34. If you slip and don't write your lunch down, but you know it was in the 5-dollar range, put $5.00. It is better than putting nothing down at all. If you round in this instance, you will be less than a dollar off, if you don't at least put a place holder for the entry, you will be more than $5 off when you look at your monthly totals.

A personal exception I take to this standard is when I am trying to break apart a receipt and figure taxes. Okay, Folks, I guess at the taxes! (There, I said it.) I do take care when I do this, however, for all my finagling to equal the total amount spent, so even though I am likely wrong about the individual categories, I am spot on with the total amount spent at Stuffmart or some tempting outlet.

Write down the amount you spend and a name of the category for your spending with each entry. For instance, I might write down Miscellaneous $3.29. Or Food $82.41.

The names and specificity of your categories are totally up to you. As a rule, they should neither be too general or too specific. After a few months of this, you will find there is a natural pattern to your categories. You will see the patterns of your buying behaviors and can get to where you know about how many categories you use with your spending.

For that one expense that is rare, or so obscure that it doesn't fit anywhere else, designate it in the "Miscellaneous" category. This is the catch-all category. It is great for collecting the oddball expenses, but beware.

Your Miscellaneous category can also become an outlet for being lazy. If your miscellaneous category is $200-$500, or more, on average each month, you need to take a look at what is going into that category. You may need to make a new category, or lump a miscellaneous expense into an existing category, if it fits at all.

Ideally, your Miscellaneous should be under $100 per month. Why? Miscellaneous tells you nothing about your spending habits other than the amount you spend. To get your self-education, you need to know a specific name of the types of items for which you are forking out cash. You may want to write a detail about the miscellaneous entry out to the side such as "(gum)" or "(postage)," so you can clearly see what the miscellaneous expense is, in case you want to make it its own category later.

Try to track expenses for 30 days. You may even decide if you are in the middle of the month to start saving receipts so that you will be in the habit already when the first of the new month comes.

So that posting receipts is not such a dreaded chore, try to take a minute at the end of the day to round up receipts and post everything daily. Trust me, the 5 or 10 minutes you spend doing it every day will feel a lot less painful than an hour or more trying to sift through one month's worth of thermal paper.

If you have shopped at Stuffmart, as most of us have, get into the habit of breaking up the receipt by category. You should not have a Stuffmart category in your budget, or any other store for that matter. Instead, if you bought laundry detergent, potato chips, and toothpaste, break that up into house, food, and personal. Take the time to do this. I doubt you'll be sorry.

Also, consider taxes. You can get by with saying you paid $599.99 for your TV, but it actually might be more like $637.82. You just skewed your numbers by $37.83. A few things like that and you have much deviation in your totals at the end of the month.

You may even go as far as my mom and I do and put your purchases on the conveyer belt in categories at the checkout lane. This is a time saver later, as all your pet supplies and hair accessories are easy to pick out on your receipt, because they were scanned through together.

But, if the store check-out clerk thwarts your progress, be gentle with them. They may make a lot less money and have a tougher day going on than you do.

When you have collected a month's worth of data, you are ready for some fun. Add up the categories, category-by-category. All the food should be totaled. All the toiletries. All the pet supplies. And, medical and miscellaneous.

Food for Thought:

Better to spend extra time deciphering UPC codes than give someone a hard time.

When you get everything totaled, take a look! You might be surprised, or horrified. This is what you spend in a month. Even with one complete month of data, you can start to see what you are really doing to yourself financially. The self-education I mentioned will kick in, and then the magic happens: you can make educated choices about your spending habits.

The second piece of paper is for totaling the categories in a list format. You will keep this second piece of paper for at least six months or more.

Every month, track expenses on one sheet, and total the categories on the other.

When you get six months worth of data, you are ready for some big-kid fun. I choose to recommend six months because most major expenses happen within those months, like insurance premiums and house repairs. Six months gives you enough time to get a truer idea about what you spend, while preserving time in the sense that you don't wait a year to start your annual budget (with fairly realistic figures).

If you have lump sum expenses, like a year's worth of auto and home insurance, or property taxes at the end of the year, consider that in your annual outlook. Also, don't forget to budget for Christmas!

So, what you will do is take out your sheets of paper with your monthly category totals on them. Total every category together (food with food for the six months of data, personal with personal, etc.) so you have a six-month total figure, then divide by six to get your average monthly expense for each category.

Also, multiply your six-month totals by two to get your yearly amount spent. The numbers you will get may leave you flabbergasted, but that is okay. Now, it is time to trim.

With your figures, you can clearly see what you are spending; and, my guess is that you can find areas in which to make cuts. You can find hundreds, even thousands, of dollars that are "fluffy" parts of your budget. Go ahead, trim, and get lean.

When you are doing your big data crunching you can also reach far ahead by doing another eye-opening exercise. Find your yearly amount spent on a habit (and it is better when it is a naughty habit, like lattes or downloaded music) and then multiply by 10.

Further picking on lattes, consider that, if you have a 5-dollar-a-day latte habit, over 10 years, it will really add up. That latte over 10 years will deprive you of $18,200. I am not kidding. Try this exercise with your gas money, your transportation costs, your gym membership, and your massages so you can see long-term what you are doing to yourself and your wallet.

> Mistakes, like a long commute, can alter your retirement plans.

When you look at big numbers like that it hits home. If your commute and your spa day will suck $89,000 out of your income over 10 years, it is easy to see that a few mistakes like that can alter your retirement plans. So go ahead, do the math. My guess is, you will see where you can trim after that.

The Lazy Budget benefits are worth the wait. Take the time to collect the data and get realistic figures for your annual outlook. The reason why I don't want you to just randomly pick amounts on the first month and go forth is because, if you choose an unrealistic number (like $25.00 for groceries for the month), you set yourself up for failure and discouragement. With realistic numbers you can know what you are dealing with, and manage your expectations accordingly.

That is why six months is highly recommended as your gauge for your yearly budget estimates. It is easy to double, and the data will likely be more sufficient than it would be with three months of data, or worse, one month of data.

With your expectations managed properly, you can set yourself up to meet your goals, or do even better than you imagined. You won't be beating yourself up when your grocery bill is $386, because you budgeted $400!

You may just decide that you want to retire early instead of feel relaxed for a few hours after a massage and facial. You may decide you want to move closer to your work. Self education is

> **Take Action:**
>
> Think of what you really want. Is it a trip? A new-to-you vehicle? Find places you can cut back so you can put your money toward your goal.

priceless, and making wise decisions in light of the data will pay you hugely in the end.

After you have your numbers and your plan to cut the fluff, it is time for the rubber to meet the road and the restoration of your wallet to begin. An important tool for simplification of finances is the art of fasting. We will talk about two kinds of fasting in this manual - spending fasts and media fasts. Both will help you save money, one directly, the other indirectly.

You have come so far! Stay with the course. There is much more to come to provide you tools for the quest of simplification. Right now, we will start with spending fasts. Go ahead, turn the page!

# Spending Fasts

No one likes the idea of deprivation. When a feeling of lack is present it steals the joy of the moment away.

Maybe that is part of what drives us to keep acquiring and getting surrounded by trinkets and trash. We don't want to be deprived.

Spending fasts may seem like self-imposed deprivation, but they are not. In fact, you may find them rather liberating and a path to abundance.

Spending fasts are a reset button for your spending. Their purpose is to take spending out of the subconscious and unconscious, where it winds up over time, and put spending back into the deliberate consciousness.

There are two ways to go about a spending fast. The first is to do a blitz on all spending. The second is to cut out an item, or a category of items. Both ways depend on the fast being done for a certain amount of time and then normal shopping is allowed again.

The blitz on all spending is something for which you will have to prepare in advance. Make sure you have groceries, and have gas for your car. It is good to make a total spending blackout for a short period of time, a few days to a week at most.

> **Food for Thought:**
>
> Even after you go back to normal spending, the effects of the spending fast will be felt. For a while, the decisions you make will still be in the arena of the deliberate and conscious. You will decide if you want that music or t-shirt. You will decide if you don't want it. It will be a well thought-out decision.

The reason for keeping it short is that we all need to buy things eventually, and poor planning and subsequent purchasing against the fast can go badly toward keeping up good morale.

The second method (which is taking out an item or a category of items) can go a little longer in duration, typically. If you are going without a latte, a week may be sufficient to open your eyes to how automated you are when you set foot in the coffee shop, or you may need to go without your specialty go-go juice for a month or more. Same goes with clothes, books, or music.

The point of the spending fast is to open your eyes to how much spending goes on without thinking things through. It's amazing how easy it is to find yourself at the neighborhood coffee shop buying a latte even after you have said, "No lattes this week." It is because our habits make us fly through life on autopilot.

There is an obvious benefit to spending fasts, too. You will be saving money! Just think about what would happen if, for a week, you cut out your $10 lunch that you buy to treat yourself for working. If, for five days, you brown-bag your lunch, that is $50 in your pocket. If you did so for a month, that is $200 in your pocket! What could you do with $200 extra?

Spending fasts are not a one-and-done deal. They are meant to be a reoccurring practice throughout your life. The effects of a spending fast aren't permanent. They need to be recharged occasionally by a fresh fast.

Keep the challenge element alive. When one thing becomes easy, change items or categories. You may also change the length of time you go without something. Switch back and forth from specific item to blitz on everything. Keep it fun, and keep it meaningful. If you know you can go your entire life without cigarettes, choose something else to fast about.

Viewing frugality as a fast rather than a lifestyle can be helpful to those who are adverse to thrift without end. The limited nature of the fast can make it seem more like a sport than a sentence. When you know you can go back to normal after a while, it is more easy to endure.

Probably, though, once you adopt spending fasts as a regular event for your life, you will find yourself edging toward greater and greater frugality. Frugality isn't deprivation. It isn't what poor people do. It is what people who want to acquire and keep wealth practice.

> Take Action:
>
> Take a moment to pick a category of item that you can do without for a week. Mark your calendar for this next week, starting now, to do without the item. Start your new habit of spending fasts today!

Now, we will switch gears from outgoing to incoming. We will talk about refraining from putting messages in our heads that will go against fostering contentment and financial conservatism. Turn the page and learn about fasting from media for an improved you!

# Media Fasts

Don't worry, we aren't going to take all your fun away! Media fasts are a way of opening your eyes to what is really going on behind the curtain of advertising. It is important to distance yourself from the media messages so that you can get control over your desires and spending.

The estimates on how many ads we see per day vary widely. Some internet sources say that we see between 300-700 ads per day. Other estimates run as high as 5,000 ads per day.[1,2]

But, even if the exact answer is unknown, there is a consensus that we are inundated with ads daily. In the post-war era after WWII, in the United States advertising took on a more visceral message: the advertisements played to basic psychological needs.

Ads before the 1950's typically would tell you what the item cost, where it could be found, and what it did. After the shift, the ad told you who you were, or who you were not, if you did or did not have the item being advertised.

Fast forward to today, when we have a culture where "belongings" equal belonging. We use products to express ourselves, and we seek out material items to improve our sense of worth and meaning.

Partaking in media fasts is a way to break the hold advertising has on your life. You won't be haunted by a supermodel seductively wearing the jeans that will bring an excited and panting Mr. Fabulous to your doorstep.  Your cookware will be able to prepare a meal regardless of the label etched into the lid handle on your stock pot.

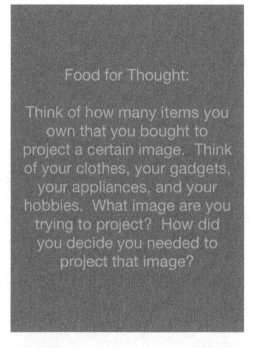

Food for Thought:

Think of how many items you own that you bought to project a certain image.  Think of your clothes, your gadgets, your appliances, and your hobbies.  What image are you trying to project?  How did you decide you needed to project that image?

It sounds radical and countercultural when you first hear it, and trust me, it is revolutionary to do it.  Turn off the TV.  That is the first major step in media fasts.  And it is one of the most important.

Further into media fasting is abstaining from magazines and maybe even internet (though I have not done the ad blocking on my browser, ever).  This self-imposed blackout sounds extreme, but here is what you get out of the deal:

You develop a heightened awareness of the real message of advertising.  You will begin to understand that the ads are not telling you what a product does, or where you can get it.  It is telling you who you are, or who you are not, if you do or do not have the item being advertised.

You will also foster having comfort in what you already have. You will begin to feel confident as you are, and accept yourself as you are, without the advertisements telling you that you are less without their product or service.

At our castle, we have one TV. It doesn't get local channels, certainly not cable, and it works hard to collect dust a great deal of the time. My husband uses it with his video game console and to watch movies.

When someone talks about ads they saw on TV, I give a blank stare. I honestly don't know what is happening on Channel 9, and I don't care.

> Food for Thought:
>
> If you have two programs that are your favorite to watch nightly, and you do not watch them, you potentially have two hours of free time just handed to you when you turn off the TV.
>
> What could you do with two extra hours a day?

I have lived this way for about ten years, and I love it. My clothes are ones I want to wear, not that I was told I needed to wear. My perfume is not endorsed by a celebrity as far as I know. My hair is styled to suit me, and is influenced by convenience.

I will be the first to admit that I am out of touch with popular culture. I don't know what the latest fashion trends are; and I don't know many celebrities that have come to fame since 2008.

But I am in touch with my own story, and my likes and dislikes. I know that I like casual clothing and pieces with versatility for my wardrobe. I prefer flats to heels. I think financial intelligence is sexy and I enjoy hearing TEDx talks about various subjects. Oh, and I can still recognize a picture of Brad Pitt, most of the time.

Try a media fast for three days if a week sounds too daunting to you. Just a small break can still be enough to reset your eyes and mind to pick up the true message of the ads that are inflicted upon us.

> **Take Action:**
>
> Unplug your TV if you live alone. If you live with someone, try to avoid the rooms with TVs that are turned on. Do this for three days.

Be in touch in your conscious mind with the lies that are put forth through marketing. You can rise up, and make better decisions for you and your family. You can yell a resounding "No" against the proposal to raid your wallet for silly goods and services that will just serve to further clutter your life.

So, we have discussed taking away to make room for better. Now, we will switch and talk about what can be added to enhance the process of becoming a sleek, simplified version of ourselves.

A tool is outlined next: the sketch-journal. This is a great place to birth creativity and reflect on progress. I have done this for years with great success, taking breaks from the discipline along the way. Keep going, you are doing great!


(1) http://blog.telesian.com/how-many-advertisements-do-we-see-each-day/

(2) https://www.cbsnews.com/news/cutting-through-advertising-clutter/

# The Sketch-Journal

(Revamped from <u>Minimize: Kill your debt. Live your dream.</u> Copyright 2013).

It is time now to introduce a tool to you that will help unlock your creativity, and help on your journey in simplifying. The tool is flexible, personal, and can be a lot of fun. You can keep it (and it is highly recommended to keep so you can chart where you've been in these travels), or discard it when it has served your purpose. It is the sketch-journal.

Your sketch-journal is yours, for your eyes only. The purpose of it is to get into a discipline of writing and drawing as only you can do. This will give you a tangible outlet to make lists; doodle; say profound, silly, or fun things; collect quotes; or wax poetic. This is instrumental in the life of someone who is decluttering because you can track progress in your mental landscape as old truths are replaced by new insights.

I started making sketchbooks when I was a preteen and continued into college. In 1996, I began journaling, and finally, I blended the two disciplines.

The rule is there are no rules. If you want, write upside down or backwards. Scribble so hard you tear holes in your paper, or spend hours on one small sketch. Make it yours.

It may work best to have a quota like one page, or three pages a day. Just free thought on paper. I personally like unlined paper the best, and treat myself to spiral-bound hardcover sketch books. Perhaps you will go weeks without drawing. Sometimes you may render several pictures at once.

Ask hard questions in your sketch-journals. "What makes me happy?" is one of my favorites and one of the ones I find hardest to answer. Make lists. "100 things I can't live without" and "free things to do" are some favorites.

A sketch-journal will keep you connected with a level of honesty. If you pour forth on paper you can go back, years later, and see what was going on in your head. This keeps the past from being romanticized or demonized.

For me, this small luxury has been priceless. I have a way of venting that is limited only by myself. My sketch-journal is there to remind me, encourage me, inspire me, and humble me.

Through journals I track my progress, stumbles, and face-plants in my continuing to become more authentically me, through simplifying. The journals also encourage me to think outside the box (perceiving more than only one solution) better than before. That definitely helps when trying to resolve a problem without buying anything new.

 My sketch-journal is used to record happenings, dream on paper, use a collage of different things that interest me (think Stone-Age Pinterest), make lists, and vent anger (those pages are usually torn out). A guttural feeling cloaks me when drawing, and it is possible to lose myself completely when rendering a sketch from whatever is available.

(I saved two of my journals and had a friend burn the rest in the early part of last year. It was a decision I thought about for years. The collection filled a rubbermaid tote and at the last was sitting in my garage, unread. I have not regretted keeping them for many years, and I did not regret letting them go. I do have a watercolor sketch book now - and the outline for this book is contained inside, as well as a list of things I needed to do around the house. So, I still use this tool, even today.)

For what use could your sketch-journal be? What conventional notions would you challenge? What would you capture on the pages? The only limit is the limit you set as to what your sketch-journal will, or won't, be.

Don't like a 9X12 sketchbook? Get a pile of post-it notes, or a voice recorder. Make your own paper. Make it the size of a large poster. Use a dry erase board.

Don't like a pen? Use watercolors, acrylics, magic markers, sharpies, glue sticks, glitter…the choice is entirely yours.

Above all, if you undertake this, have fun. It's a good bet that you will find more dimensions of yourself in the process.

Vision Setting

Something you want to do that is not written down is just a wish, my business manager at work tells me. When you write it down, it becomes a goal.

In addition to having the daily goal previously discussed of your most important task, I encourage you to have a life goal - this is like your mission statement. This goal is what you want your life to be about from this point forward.

Set goals for yourself in three phases. Short-, medium-, and long-term. This is not my original idea. Goal setting has been around a long, long time. But, it is definitely worth mentioning.

Your short-term goals should support your medium-term goals, and your medium-term goals should feed your long-term goals. Imagine several creeks supporting a few rivers, and those few rivers flowing into an ocean (your mission). That is what your goals should strive to do. If that mutual support is not accomplished, you will have a confused mix of efforts and the mission won't be achieved as written.

> **Take Action:**
>
> Create a rough draft of your mission statement. Make several practice mission statements until you find the one that resonates with you.

All goals must support the mission (whatever it may be) and all goals have some common characteristics. A goal that works will be:

- specific,
- measurable,
- achievable,
- consistent,
- and listed in order of importance for the mission.

(Let's look at those characteristics to expand them for understanding.)

Try to get your goals as specific as possible. A useless goal (a wish) might look like:

"Get rid of extra stuff."

That could be the end game of your effort but it isn't a usable or operational goal to get, and it won't keep you on track during the long, and frequently interrupted, journey to completion of the mission.

A better goal might look like:

"Have a first purge of my apartment completed by the first of June, 2019."

Why is this better? Because, at the first of June 2019, you will have the purge done or you won't. This goal is specific and measurable. (You have answered the "What" and "When" of those pesky "W" questions.)

You can begin working toward the next and perhaps larger goal, or, you have to set a new deadline for the first step (goal). This type of goal setting holds you accountable to you. No excuses. You own the success or failure, to make progress.

Yep, it stinks, but it will get you to the mission in a direct line or to realization that the idea won't work as conceived. And, it will do so with a minimum of time and effort while staying out of a sinking muddle. Then your time, energy, talent, and treasure have not been wasted.

That's a bad feeling, my friends, so be careful upfront. Planning pays off. My dad has a saying that reportedly originated in the U.S. Marines, edited slightly here for general audiences. It is: Prior Planning Prevents Poor Performance." The six P's of the Corps, edited to the five P's here in this manual…says it for careful planning.

Keeping with the example of purging, a short-term goal might look like:

"Declutter a drawer a day for the next week."

Short-term goals should be able to be executed (achieved) within a week to a month, ideally. They should be easy enough that you can attain them with moderate, steady effort, also known as: doing the job. These short-term goals are means to get to medium-term goals and should not be a marathon, or take a huge bundle of energy and/or time to complete.

Medium-term goals for purging might look like this:

"Have the attic, garage, and basement cleaned by March" (and it is January now).

"Have a 25% reduction in belongings by September" (and it is April now).

"Have the house, car, and outbuilding completely decluttered by November" (and it is June now).

Medium-term goals should be more marathon-esque. You should not be able to complete them quickly, and they should require determination and effort. Ideally, you should be able to complete them between three months and a year from your creation of them.

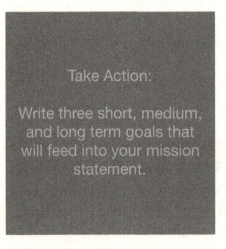

Take Action:

Write three short, medium, and long term goals that will feed into your mission statement.

Long-term goals might look like this:

"Have a 60% reduction in belongings by the third year of decluttering."

Or,

"Have all my worldly belongings fit in a

backpack by the end of my fifth year of decluttering."

Long-term goals are the heavy ones. The really big accomplishments that will take moxie and grit for perhaps years to come. They are your big plans, that feed into your life goal. Ideally, you should aim for their completion in one to five years, depending on the mission, research required, your health, and your ability/talent to complete such a mission.

Along the way, you will need to reward yourself. This holds true to your decluttering and financial goals. A word about rewards though: they should not set you back in your overall goals.

So, if you are decluttering, reward yourself with experiences or materials to help you declutter. A walk or bike ride is great. Or an e-book, if you just feel you must buy something.

If you are retiring your debt, think cheap or free. Fix a cup of tea and allow yourself five hours of leisure time. Give yourself a night away from the kids (swap babysitting services with a friend who has kids of their own). Go for a picnic.

Use your creativity to come up with rewards that will motivate you and leave you feeling satisfied. As your desires reduce and recede, it will take less and less big ticket stuff to give you a high, and make you feel treated in the right way.

So concludes our quick and dirty lesson on goal setting. Next up is authentic living. And, it takes a twist or two that you might not expect. You are doing a fantastic job of devouring this book. Keep it up! There is more, much more ahead!

# Authenticity

Authenticity is a buzzword, and a concept worth delving into when undergoing simplification.

When you are purging, you have a chance to be authentic, or honest, about what you need, what you like, and what you will wear. If you know yourself to prefer flats, ask yourself: what am I doing with stiletto heels? If you like jeans and tennis shoes, why hang on to the cocktail dress that you haven't worn since the Clintons ran the White House?

Let the stuff that you don't like, go. This certainly applies to clothes, and it also applies to almost anything you own. Strive to have things that are in congruence with your way of life now and your values. Let go of the hobby equipment you have no more interest in - and won't have it re-energized in your heart. Don't think about how much money you spent. Smell the freedom when you let it all go.

> **Food for Thought:**
>
> Keep the things that tell a story - your story - and let the rest go.

Now, to revisit a point of minimalist philosophy that we touched on a few chapters ago - you are not your stuff. You are not your collections. Having art supplies won't make you an artist, but practicing drawing and sculpting will. Having a stack of books won't make you an intellectual, but having in-depth conversations with other folks and actually reading various materials will.

You are not fashionable with trendy, flimsy pieces in your wardrobe.  You are stylish when you know what you like, it fits your body well (and this does include the art of camouflage) and you can wear what you own with confidence.  You are not a movie buff when you have a shelf completely packed with DVDs; but, when you consume a movie - watching it without collecting a trinket - you may be moving closer to being an aficionado.

For the books, DVDs, and clothes even, you may want to argue with me and say you don't just buy these things for yourself, but you buy them to share with others.  Okay.  Pause with me a moment, and recollect your feelings you had when you loaned out a book or movie and didn't get it back, or worse yet discovered that your friend had the item for months and maybe even more than a year, and still hadn't watched or read it.

This is an alternative to that feeling:  for your friends that are able to do for themselves and purchase their own stuff, recommend your favorites to them, and then wait to see if they jump and buy a copy for themselves.  If they will spend their own money on the item, they are more willing to consume it (read or watch it) and they are showing a genuine interest in it.  Trust me, this will save you some hard feelings.

Have in your home what is useful and/or beautiful to you. Wear your clothes with the same approach. No one else can be you in this universe. You owe it to yourself to be honest with yourself and others about what you like and what you don't like and of which you don't want to be a part.

When you get your calendar under control, you can choose to participate in activities that are meaningful and in line with your values. To get to that point, you need to be authentic (also known as growing a backbone).

You need to come to grips with the notion that it is better to be a little offensive and protect your time (just say, "no", firmly and tactfully) than to let yourself be swayed to participate in an activity or committee that you have no interest in, and that you resent.

You may tell me that you cannot shirk work obligations, and I may tell you depending on your finances that you may be quite right, or quite wrong.

If your finances are dire and you are up to your armpits in debt, I will tell you that you are right. If you are in slavery to your creditors, you do need to take great care to preserve your income streams. But, if you are debt free, your income streams will be important, but not imperative, and you can have some choice in whether you will work extra or attend company dinners.

A perfect example of this is a person who was working full-time at a very successful corporation. He was expected to travel, sometimes out of state, at the company's whim. He was expected to attend company functions that sometimes kept him out until after 9 PM on a weeknight. He was expected to work weekends and sometimes 12 hour days if there was a business need.

When he was in debt, this was just the way it was. There was no escape and no choice. However, this same person retired his debt, and built enough savings that he could stay out of the workforce for more than five years without changing his spending habits. That padding was a game changer.

He negotiated a deal with his employer to become a different kind of class of worker. His employer now would not ask him to travel or work weekends. He has not been expected to attend company functions to keep him out late. He was asked to work a weekend, and he did. After that weekend, he told his boss he was going back to his regular schedule, and he has done exactly that.

Not being poor gives you choices. Being fully funded gives you bargaining power. Having a stash of funds to back your backbone makes you able to negotiate a better deal for yourself. I cannot adequately express how getting out of debt and building personal wealth will open up your opportunities in life. Wealth will help you live authentically, not in the sense of buying you all the right "rich" trappings, but it will help buy you choices.

Money further assists authenticity when you have a fully funded "Stuff it!" fund. This is when you have six months to a year of expenses stashed away. The "Stuff it!" fund is not a vacation fund. It is what you will use to keep from becoming homeless in the event you have to walk away from your job. It is not a fund to replace your car either. That is a separate fund.

This fund, when mature, will allow you to be able to tell your employer "Stuff it!" if they ask you to do something that goes against your principles. This will buy you comfort knowing you can be ethical at all times, and you don't have to do something illegal or immoral, ever, on your job. A "Stuff it!" fund can give you a great sense of power and control and help you hold your head up high even on difficult days. The ability to be able to slide your name badge across the desk

> **Take Action!**
>
> Start your "Stuff It!" Fund: Put 25 dollars a week away in an account that you will not touch. In a month, you will have $100.00. In a year, you will have over $1,000.00. As you go on, add more than the minimum. When you retire your debts, you can build this fund very quickly. A couple had theirs fully funded six months after being debt free, starting with just a few hundred dollars, and that was collecting up to $10K.

at a moment's notice, gather your things, and cut ties completely is a great sense of comfort.

There are few moments more unsettling than waking up to the realization that you have been spending time, money, and effort to buy your way and conform your way to an image that you have no interest in and is not where your heart lies.

There was a time that I was buying for the "fantasy me," and not the "real me." At the end, I had a $1200 road bike, fancy spandex workout clothes, and countless butt-numbing hours on a bike saddle because I thought I needed to be athletic to earn love. Further, about the same time, I looked around my house and I didn't see me in my possessions, I saw magazine ads from home decor magazines. It was humbling.

Now my family pictures adorn the walls, not Chinese symbols I can't even read. My husband's handiworks are on the shelves of the built-in that is in our dining room (he made me a model of a Nissan Z - my favorite car ever - and a ceremonial tea hut out of popsicle sticks); and I joke with people that I give the tour to (but I am serious at the same time) that I have the house, the car, and the man of my dreams.

My belongings help tell my story, but that is not the real me. The real me is defined by my relationships — how I treat family, my friends, strangers, pets, stray animals, and even my one houseplant (though

I ask that you not judge me solely by the care of my aloe plant), and the kindnesses I dish out as well as the heartache I bring (I am not perfect, you know).

I am not: what I own, wear, drive, and live under. Neither are you.

We are taking a turn in our journey to a special topic: Sharing. When I first started reading finance books I was amazed to see giving as a topic in almost every book I read. Now I know why. It is truly the cherry on top of the wealth building experience.

You are doing a fantastic job so far of listening and considering! Keep going!

# Sharing

(Adapted from <u>Minimize: The Great Interior</u> Copyright 2014)

In simplifying, sharing is encouraged. When undertaking the "Big Purge" see who can take your castaway items. This practice is definitely encouraged to prevent unwanted items from going to the dump as you clean out your dwelling.

Inside the depths of the purge, be thoughtful. If you know that other friends and family members are trying to clean out, don't give them stuff to use them as a conduit. I came horribly close to offending and ruining a friendship with a dear gal when I was cleaning out. My friend would dutifully take my castoffs; but she later confessed that it was a burden to her. My friend is now in the process of cleaning out her own home, and much of my "donations/gifts" are walking out her door.

Granted, when you are cleaning out, it is the items of little value to you that you give away. That can't be helped; and it is healthy to divest yourself of things that do not matter to you anymore. My friend got what didn't matter to me, and it was to such an extent that she made comments that let me know she was feeling like a "Castoff Queen."

To avoid making your loved ones feel like "Castoff Queens" (and "Kings"), try to arrange it so it seems like their idea to take your belongings. Invite a group of people all at once to pick through your stuff. Have a garage sale, or several garage sales, to divest yourself of stray furniture, knickknacks, and small appliances. Be selective about what you give to others, and try to be clear in your own mind that what you intend to give will be something that can truly be of use to that person.

However, as you get more simple in your household, hopefully something will happen. You will not give out of what is meaningless and burdensome. Instead, you will give out of what matters. This is a more worthy form of giving. Using a friend as a junk conduit may bring relief to you that stuff is gone, but if it's not useful (and needed) by your friend, it can't really be helpful, since it isn't.

> Food for Thought:
>
> Not my idea originally. Credit goes to Betsy and Warren Talbot who wrote <u>Dream. Save. Do.</u>: Have a reverse birthday party! Invite your friends over to go through your castoff stuff. Serve treats and refreshments and make it a party atmosphere. If there are disputes about who should take an item home, make the ones who want the item tell a wild, made-up story about how the item came to be in their possession, and the group can vote on with whom the item will go home! Or, draw straws.

It is the difference between giving someone your navy pantsuit because you don't want it anymore, and giving someone your navy pantsuit because it fits them. (Or, maybe they have a job interview!) You know that if the need arose for you, an alternative solution could be found to the same problem.

In the first instance, the pantsuit has little value. In the second instance, giving the pantsuit is a sacrifice, and the suit has value to you still. This second scenario is a higher form of sharing.

Hopefully, when you are devoid of excess, you will use your abundance to share with others. I give gifts little and big, and it feels great. Rarely do I give my castoffs as presents or offer them up thinking I am doing a great favor.

Now, I try to share of myself. CJ does this as well. We make salsa for friends and family to take home. When we bake, we share the goods. When I bought a box of ugly tomatoes (ones with defects) this summer for $10 at a farmers' market, my parents, my neighbor, and a friend also got part of the bounty.

I give my time, also. I make sure to spend time with my parents. I see my mom and dad at least once a week on average. I also give my time to teaching others about simplification and the benefits of cleaning out and getting out of debt.

We also give money to people in need. We personally knew a hurricane victim in Florida so we sent several hundred dollars to them. We have given thousands to a relative to help them rebuild their life after a nasty divorce.

I don't believe in giving as though I am taxed by God. I don't give ten percent each month. Sometimes I give way less. Sometimes I give way more. I believe the children of the King are free, and I believe that giving is a spiritual discipline and people who withhold good from others are doing it to their own hurt.

I do think that if you belong to a religious organization (or a secular one for that matter) and they require a percent from their members, you should give the percent required to the local church or organization. No one likes a free loader. If you don't like it, perhaps it is time to rethink your membership.

> Take Action:
>
> Select ten things you own that you really are not fond of anymore but someone else might like. Ask your friends or family that might want them if they will take them. Make a plan to get those items to their new owners!

Giving is central to happiness. We are wired to give and share. When we withhold goods and services we feel a deep sense of guilt and shame. Enjoy giving. Try to give where it counts, and where it will be needed and appreciated.

You have come so far! This section was taken from my second book, <u>MInimize: The Great Interior</u>, and years later I can't really say it a whole lot better than how I wrote it the first time. Next up is gratitude, also taken from <u>The Great Interior</u>. Keep going; you are doing great!

# Gratitude

(Revamped from <u>Minimize: The Great Interior</u>. Copyright 2014)

My husband's grandfather, Pappo, is a pro at maintaining joy and gratitude. He reminds his family often of the blessings they have, and how good (in comparison to what others may have), a life in the United States can be. (He usually will put me into remembrance of little reasons to be thankful followed by his trademark giggle.)

Pappo knows about blessings. He has lived in the same community for most of his life, with Nana, his wife of over 50 years. They are pillars in the community. Pappo visits with those at his table and just about every other table in the local diner. He knows people, and they know him.

> **Food for thought:**
>
> Gratitude can make a little feel like a lot. It is related to contentment, and discontent cannot co-exist with it. Gratitude has a lot to do with feeling prosperous, and is a powerful tool in making what you have sufficient for your needs.

Something happens within us when we are grateful for what we have. Our thankfulness coincides with a feeling of abundance. Suddenly, the meal we have had seems enough without a mega-sized frozen custard, complete with bits of our favorite candy bar.  The outfit we have on is adequate to wear on our errand running; and, we might have an outfit already in our closet that we can wear to dinner with our loved one.

Our homes, our cars, our pastimes, all fall into harmony with gratitude.  When we are thankful for our shelters, the fact that the tiles in the bathroom are coming unglued seems slightly less terrifying.  When we are thankful for having a car that works dependably, it matters less that it is not a Ferrari.  When we are content with our hobbies, what the celebrities are up to seems worlds away and far removed from our own sense of happiness.

Cultivate gratitude.  It is not something that is expected to happen automatically, or be persistent without prodding.  Make an effort to be content.  Think about the good angles of your circumstances.  Focus on what is right in your life, and seek to add to that collection of events and people.

This is not to say go blithely in the face of difficulty.  Be aware of your challenges, but not to the point of being consuming.  You will have dark days, but don't stay there in the abyss of self-pity and consternation.

Look for opportunity in the midst of difficulty.  Stop saying, "I can't," and instead ask, "How can I?"  A crisis is uncomfortable, to be sure, but it is not crushing.

Gratitude plays a role in a comeback. A person who has an active list of things they are grateful for has something to fall back on when an area of their life is out-of-whack.

Let's take, for example, when a job turns sour, or is lost. If a person is grateful for their families, their hobbies, and what life has afforded them, the loss of the job is viewed differently, less centrally, than someone who has nothing on which to fall back.

Being able to find pleasure in small things is such a gift. One past winter there were several days in a row that snow did not permit easy travel. During those times there were days and days of staying at home. My husband was able to entertain himself; and, I was able to keep busy, too. I journaled, daydreamed, and cooked at home.

If you are trying to tame debt, gratitude can be a powerful ally. If you are not lusting after what the Joneses have, what you have seems enough. You may find yourself taking pleasure in coming up with thrifty solutions to your problems. If you can be content with what you have, you are not as ready to chase after those things that you do not have.

For my personal battle with debt and gratitude, I must confess to you that I have taken steps forward as well as backward. My father is kind enough to keep me humble, making sure to point out any and all hypocrisy that he finds tumbling within me.

When I wrote <u>Minimize: Kill your debt. Live your dream.</u>, I was still eating out on a frequency. So was my husband. Finally, in a cold December, we buckled down and started consistently eating at home. The difference was astounding! What was an 800-dollar per month food bill before, dropped to $386!

As in <u>Minimize</u>, it is recommended to approach gratitude as a discipline. Make a list, or several lists, of things for which you are thankful. Refer back to these lists in difficult or dark times. The items may not all hold true for you in depressed states, but a few will pop out as being relevant and right.

New to listing out things for which you are thankful? Start with ten things. They can be whatever you want, so long as you are being genuine. Your Mom is your anchorwoman? Put her on the list. Toothpaste the greatest thing ever? On the list it goes!

Don't worry if you think of only seven things. This is an exercise that you will hopefully repeat again and again. Building gratitude is a lot like building muscle. One great big workout doesn't give you fabulous abs. It is the consistent, stretching, faithful practice that will get you to a list of 100 things or more, and have you shivering out of joy in the middle of the night.

To be fair, I did the exercise myself. It stands to reason that you shouldn't be expected to do something that I did not do myself. So, here goes. One hundred things I am thankful for today (and I did leave this list and come back to it, so don't think you have to do it all in one sitting).

THINGS FOR WHICH I AM THANKFUL (2018)
1. God
2. Mom and Dad
3. my husband
4. Chia (the cat)
5. employment
6. my friends
7. Gizzy and Cali (RIP)
8. that I am eating mostly at home
9. that we are debt free
10. that TJ Maxx does not captivate me
11. that Pier 1 doesn't either
12. Mr. Money Mustache
13. that my house is minimized
14. that our goal is not to get a bigger house
15. that we can work part-time
16. that I can provide medical care for my cat
17. nomoreharvarddebt.com
18. Miss Minimalist
19. my tiffany lamp
20. people who will go out of their way to be a friend
21. that God listens to my prayers
22. General Tso's Chicken
23. my Bible study buddies
24. people who challenge me
25. people who humble me

26. failure
27. screened-in porches
28. that God sometimes tells me "no"
29. the ability to walk
30. a good cupcake (or two)
31. that both of my parents are living
32. that my spouse is living
33. I do not live in a war zone
34. that I have access to medical care
35. that I enjoy reasonably good health
36. that I can go on a bike ride in the spring
37. fall leaves
38. crisp autumn air
39. the smell of fallen leaves
40. blooming trees
41. really, blooming anything!
42. my in-laws
43. that my cat makes me laugh
44. toothpaste
45. computers
46. internet
47. fuzzy socks
48. blinds on the windows of my home
49. Chai tea
50. waterproof mattress covers
51. less-packaged items at Lucky's Market
52. SOAP refill station in downtown Springfield
53. my car
54. that my car is currently running
55. comfortable footwear
56. creativity through writing and painting
57. watercolors
58. the way God took care of me during a car wreck

59. the way he takes care of me daily
60. evenings at home
61. evenings with friends
62. my fuzzy robe
63. apartment pants
64. flowers that bloom in unfavorable weather
65. the way cameras come on phones now
66. my smartphone
67. that I know CJ loves me
68. that we get much time together in the evenings
69. private property
70. private thoughts
71. garlic (it makes a blah dish taste great!)
72. cooking with red wine
73. ice cream
74. that I can pursue my dreams
75. that there is currently not anarchy where I live
76. modern art
77. Bansky and others like him
78. conscientious people
79. polite people
80. the experience of marketing my first three books
81. being able to present on simplification
82. SAM's Club
83. bulk coffee
84. the ability to daydream
85. the ability to journal
86. the Sistine Chapel and other works like it
87. that my mother and I have a good relationship
88. that my father and I have grown closer
89. the Kindle App
90. a year with adequate rain
91. celebrating birthdays

92. free food
93. that right now I can pay my bills
94. that I had enough money to pay my taxes
95. gummy bears
96. my patients at work and their stories
97. helping people for a profession
98. that I am an introverted soul
99. that I am not forgetting too much...yet
100. for life, breath, and all things

Not thankful for your relationship with your sister? Don't put it on the list! Thankful for that macrame towel holder Aunt Edna gave you? Put that sucker on the list near the top! The trick in this is to be genuine. You will always know when you are trying to deceive yourself.

> Take Action:
>
> Get a pen and piece of paper and write 10 things you are thankful for. Do this exercise for the next 5 days.

Respect yourself enough that you have a level of emotional honesty always present. Not thankful that you got fired from your job? Don't go around faking it hoping that you'll make it. Instead, keep in touch with what you are thankful for in life. It may be a big thing. It may be a small thing. Find it, and hang on to it. You will be so glad you did.

Now, I have saved the best for last. True stories coming up about the real magic of involving God on your quest for simplification. Keep reading, the most important chapter (in my opinion) is coming up!

# Involve God

The further in my walk with God I go, the more dependent I am on him for the most mundane things. I like to involve him in much in my life, from major decisions to helping find motivation to clean the bathroom.

He is there for me, and is a very good help. I fancy that he entertains my prayers about common things to get me to dream about what he would provide if I put his kingdom first, and asked for things to advance Heaven and not necessarily my daily agenda. I am in the process of figuring out what happens with that request.

I wanted to share some stories with you from my life about involving God in the process of decorating and minimizing. These are true, and it goes to show how God humors our little requests.

The Bedroom

When we were in the race to retire the mortgage, I had a queen-sized bed in my very tiny bedroom. It took up almost the whole room. There was barely room for two night stands by the bed and a tall, skinny, lingerie chest in the corner.

When we would pass through this room, especially in the dark of night, often we would bang our hips into the footboard of the bed as we travelled onward to the front of the house.

I wanted to redo this room. I was very specific about what I wanted: a twin-sized mattress resting on shipping pallets, new sheets for the new-sized bed, a throw for decor at the end of the bed, new curtains, a new curtain rod (and I wanted a stick devoid of limbs for a natural, quirky look), I wanted an area rug, also.

And, I wanted everything to cost me $100, or less, out-of-pocket money.

I turned my gaze heavenward and said to the effect, "Want to help me with this one?" I gave God my budget, and then waited.

The next day I was riding my bike down my street and I saw a garage sale. There, propped on a realtor's sign, was my curtain rod. It was a walking stick, and I picked it up for $5.

So, now, I was at $95 for my budget. My mom agreed to help me turn my queen-size, flat sheet into gray tab curtains so the curtains were solved for free. (We did an awesome job on that project, by the way. Mom was super about knowing what to do to make it look good.)

The pallets didn't come and didn't come. I got impatient and started looking at prices for them at Home Depot. Over $100, so not an option.

My dad was wrapping up a divorce and moved into an older bungalow with a basement about this time.

In the basement was... yes...pallets! I chose the two I wanted and brought them home in my hatchback.

For the mattress, I was very specific: I wanted a pillow-top. I looked and looked for one. For my birthday, I received $150 dollars of play money. I looked one night on Amazon and found one - for just a few dollars less than my limit. Did I click the order button? You bet I did.

The area rug was also an Amazon item, and I put the one I wanted on a watch list. It started at around $100 and began dropping in price. When one day I noticed it was $61, and some change, I sprang for it. That was the most expensive out-of-pocket expense of the adventure.

The throw and the sheets were bought with rewards points from my credit card. I did have to put some money toward them, but not much. I also bought curtain tie-back hooks to use as holders for my walking stick/curtain rod.

I kept track of the money I spent, and when the project was finished, I had spent barely under $100. When people come to my house I tell them the story, even though I have done some redecorating since this adventure took place.

It took some waiting and some patience. I believe, from beginning to end, the project took about eight months to complete. But, it was worth it.

The Mattress

One of the adjustments the room has gone through is acquiring a new mattress.  The one I got from Amazon felt like sleeping on a cinderblock by 7:00 AM about six months after it was installed.  I endured for many more months - actually a few years.

At the beginning of a very tight year - when I was going part-time - I looked heavenward and said to God that I didn't feel like spending big bucks on a mattress, but I would appreciate a new one nevertheless.

God listened.

I was having lunch at work with a dear friend not long after.  "Do you know of anyone needing a mattress?" she asked.  My ears perked up and through a mouthful of food I asked, "What size is it?"

One of the drawbacks of the Amazon mattress was it was a regular twin length.  I am tall, and it always bugged me that my feet hung off the end when I slept on my stomach.

"Twin XL" my friend replied.

I became very, very excited.  As it worked out, I got a mattress that had been protected in a cover and was in pristine condition.  It was a pillow top, and has been worlds more comfortable than the old mattress.

My friend delivered it to my house, and I gave her a couple of gift cards that had been given to me, as a token for it, because she refused to charge me for it. I am still sleeping comfortably (and with my feet on the mattress) to this day. I did buy new sheets for the new-sized mattress. My mom gave me a mattress cover for it.

The Jacket

When I had downsized my wardrobe, I wanted to get a black jacket (light-weight to medium-weight). I needed this thing to shed cat hair with my two lovelies (cats) at home producing fur like it was going out of style.

I knew North Face brand would have what I wanted, but I didn't want to pay for one new. I hunted around at thrift stores but didn't find what I needed. I had it on my radar for over a year.

One fine day I was at Goodwill. I was looking for the jacket of my dreams but wasn't finding it. I began to pray (and I am not kidding about this); and I wandered over to a rack of clothes that had not been put out yet and started running my hands through the pieces of fabric.

My hand hit something. The something. I knew it was the fabric I wanted and the weight I wanted. I pulled out a black jacket. It was my jacket.

It was a good fit, it was the color I wanted, it had a hood as a bonus, and was a Champion brand jacket! I paid...$4.50 for this find.

I think that God is supportive of thrift and frugality. When I have buckled down, and have not wanted to spend, he has repeatedly given me little gifts that I know are from him.

> **Take Action:**
>
> Ask God to reveal himself to you. If you truly mean it, and you really want to know him and are ready to accept the truth about him and Jesus, He will guide you into all truth. Keep seeking; you will keep finding.

So, needing to decorate or do a little shopping? Involve the Holy of Holies on your adventure is my advice. When he gives you your desire, it may not be exactly what you envisioned, but it will get the job done.

Remember to tell him "thank you." He is a fan of gratitude from his kids.

This concludes the sections on tools. You are getting close to finishing this book! Kudos to you for sticking it out this far. Next will be some wrap-up sections and some parting thoughts. At the end are some resources and appendices for your perusal.

You are doing great!

# Spouses, Significant Others, and Roommates

(Adapted from <u>Minimize: Kill your debt. Live your dream.</u> Copyright 2013.)

Your live-in loved ones may be a hinderance or a help in your quest to simplify. They may seem off their rocker in their protests of cleaning out; but, keep the following in mind before you try to claim the moral high ground.

> You have little idea of the fear you are able to inflict upon your loved ones when you start clearing a swath through the home you share with them.

My husband stood by in amazement as I began purging twice a year. He was kind enough to not protest, but occasionally he would ask me if I threw something out that was his when he couldn't find it. Actually, he still does to this day.

Somehow, our sense of selves and our marriage have survived nearly nine years of purging and minimizing. My husband has made great strides in accepting me, and the way I wish to live; and, he is even embracing and spearheading the leadership in our family in frugal money philosophy. The alternatives are unacceptable to both of us, so I am very grateful.

While we still disagree on things like appropriate square footage, we have had a meeting of the minds about purchasing a home with cash, with modest square footage. CJ was willing to not go in debt again for a larger home, and we now live in a paid-for, small bungalow.

I decided early on not to invade his personal areas, like his Man Lair and car, with my cleaning and clearing frenzy; and, in August of 2013, he gave me such a big reward by cleaning out his Man Lair closet - completely voluntarily. And, then, he sold nearly 80 percent of his DVD and video game collection! In the years since, he has not re-accumulated very much at all. We download movies now and CJ watches streaming services for his favorite shows.

If you are alone in your quest to minimize, take heart! Meet your loved one head-on with patience and understanding. It's not easy to watch a change, and it is sure not easy when it is under the same roof.

It is important to talk about the issue. Talk with your loved one rather than to them. Don't lecture, just explain briefly, and be the change you wish to see in the world. I recommend keeping away from their personal items or things they brought into the relationship (but your things are fair game).

My husband is not controlling. I did not consult him when I got rid of some wedding presents. I did not consult him when I downsized the dishes or the kitchen items. I did not need to. The house is decorated the way I chose. (You might say I am the controlling one.)

I tried to respect his turf. I did not throw away any of his clothes (except for underwear with holes) without his consent. I did not touch the Man Lair closet for two years, even though I would have liked to very much, *very much indeed.*

Communication is key to success. You will never know what lies in the heart of your loved one unless you ask. I still have conversations with CJ during which I ask him what he dreams of doing and being. I ask him how I can help him become what he wants to be, and I think he knows that I am supportive of him and his adventures.

In return, he listened to me when I said that I didn't want my life's goal to be owning a bigger home. He heard me when I said I don't want more debt, and the philosophy has caught fire in him as well. One day, we may get a bigger home (he is still adamant that he wants more square footage), but perhaps we won't wind up in a financial mess to get it.

I have never had a cross word from my husband about working part-time during the two times in my married life that I have had less than full-time employment. He urged me not to go back working full-time the first time, but the decision was in my hands and I wanted to pitch in to get our debt demolished more quickly. He knows that pursuing creativity was something I wanted to try. He saw the opportunity with me, and did not fault me at all for the times that I contributed less income.

What to keep in mind, if your spouse, roommate, or significant other is not on board with the minimizing project, is this: Meet them head-on with love and understanding. It is not easy to watch someone adopt a new philosophy and lifestyle that you don't agree with, or want a part of for yourself.

Meet them head-on with love and understanding.

They may not get that simplification is about having more, not less. They may not get that "more" (in the case of simplifying) would mean more opportunities to pursue your dreams, and "less" is less knickknacks and dependency on a job you hate, to pay for things you don't need and love.

If you go about it sensibly and compassionately, you will see progress with your spouse/significant other/roommate. Simplifying is contagious. I think it is catching because there is truth in it. Be the change you wish to see in the world, and lead by example, not nagging, or ultimatums you won't want to, or can't, back up with action.

This is mainly applicable to adults in the household. So, what about kids? Keep going, that section is next. Written by two dear friends with wee-ones, you will get tested and true strategies and advice for downsizing and frugal living with an active family. Keep going, you are doing great!

# Kids and Decluttering

There are two strategies that I know of to try on wee-ones that need to let go of their loot: bribing and guilting. This is spoken by a person who is childless, so you may want to take it with a grain of salt. But, wait!

If you continue to read, you will hear from mothers that have spent time and effort in the process of making their homes streamlined, simplified, and frugal. Tara and Beth pitched in to help make this book more well-rounded and relevant, and my own mom wanted me to include her creative way of foregoing the toy store.

Without getting rid of your child's toys, or buying another one for Junior, you can keep the interest fresh for your child. (This same strategy can be used with adults and their knickknack collections.)

Marilyn, my dear mom, would, when I was a youngster, go through my room and bag up half of my toys and their various little parts. (Half, not all, of my toys!) She would put them in grocery sacks and put them in my closet, out of reach of my little arms and hands.

Then, she would let time pass. About six months or so would go by and then she would bring out the other half of my toys and bag the half I had been playing with in those same grocery sacks.

The result? I was never bored with my toys. It was a windfall twice a year of fresh stuff to play with during the daytime hours. Mom saved a bundle, and I never complained about the arrangement. Win-win.

* * *

Now, to share the two strategies that I believe will work with future generations.

Bribing

When trying to get a mini-hoarder to let go of their stuff, see if you can appeal to their sense of greed. Give them the option to give you 15 or 20 (or, whatever number you decide) of their toys they are tired of, and no longer want, in exchange for one nice new toy of their choice (within reason).

That's a 15:1 ratio, Mom and Dad! Go for it. If you wind up buying six toys you will have parted with 90 odds and ends out of Junior's room. Think of the possibilities!

Guilting

If you are raising a kind-hearted and gentle child, try guilting them into letting go of toys. Tell them that their toys they no longer want and use can be used by someone else in the community, or overseas, that has fewer, or no, toys like your child has. Involve them in selecting what goes, and let them help you box it up and deliver it to your local charity outlet. You will be fostering good habits in them and when they are adults, they will know how to properly offload!

That is what I know. But, listen to the advice of two wonderful friends of mine. Tara, a mother of a nine-year-old, and Beth, a mother of a pre-teen and teenager. They are able to report straight from the trenches.

* * *

Here is advice from Tara. (Edited for flow.) She writes:

Our dear children come into this world with nothing. Zilch. Nada. The doctor hands the mom and dad the precious bundle of joy and then for the next 18-25 years they live with us and we shower them with stuff.

He needed the baby blankets and clothes (60 baby onesie/outfits from the baby shower alone. Yes, 60!). He needed the developmental toys, the big diaper bag, small diaper bag, that cool stroller, the boppy, the swing, the rocker, the highchair, the walker, the bassinet, and crib (of course). Oh, we can't live without the car seats for each car and the breast pump. That gets us through year number one.

From there, it's a mountain of toys, clothes, sporting events…and did I mention toys? Lord help us if it's the first grandchild! Those grandparents, aunts and uncles, and friends help add to the toy pile.

My beautiful baby came into the world with nothing; and, suddenly, in one year, his belongings had filled up half my house. But, he NEEDED all those things.

Right?

Let's talk for a bit. Does my child need 200 action figures? Well, mine thinks he does. Does he need 24 puzzles? Well, he thinks he does. How about the 65 shirts that are short sleeve shirts that currently fit? Sure, he needs them. Or, does he? He needs food. He needs shelter. Mostly, he needs my love and attention.

I recently moved from a 1200 square-foot home to a 825 square-foot home. I moved from a four-bedroom house to a two-bedroom house. My son has spent his first 9 years in that four-bedroom house and we acquired a lot!

He had an entire room as a "playroom" and then also had his bedroom for some more toys, books, and his mounds of clothing. We had to drastically scale it down. I knew in his new room he'd have to fit all his bedroom stuff, as well as his playroom stuff, into one room. He wasn't excited about moving and sure wasn't excited about giving up everything he knew....like his rooms and his toys. So, drastic measures had to happen.

I've read many ways on how to clean a kid's room, how to get them involved, how to minimize and how to have some sort of order. There are many ways out there, and they are as vast as the personalities of each child.

I love organizing, and had tons of bins and boxes for his toys. I made a rule that if you pull it out, you play with it, then pick up that bin before getting the next bin out. A beautiful idea, in theory. After the newness wore off he was back to dragging tons of toys out and not keeping them organized.

One thing I read said to do the purging while the child isn't home. I'm not a fan of that. My son cares about his belongings like I care about mine. Sure, I own them, but I am trying to teach my child love, respect, and being honest. I can't do something hateful and dishonest and expect him to not remember my example.

My son had so much. I'm embarrassed to say how much. His rooms were rarely clean and if they got clean it ended up being a big argument. There were always tears involved from him or from me.

One day, I decided to give him an offer. I offered him $20 if he'd give away 40 items to children in need. Money talked. He was all-in on this deal. Suddenly, parting with the toys he didn't play with every day became easy.

I told him to find all the fast-food toys and put them in a box. We gave the box to a local church where they were able to use the toys. The deal I made with him was that he could use the money or save the money. We had the understanding he could take the money and turn around and buy ONE toy. His decision.

After it was over (he purged those toys in lightening speed), I took the toys to second-hand shops and gave other toys to friends.

But, he still had too many toys!

We decided to give books to the library and to teachers' classrooms. For the toys that went in our garage sale, I offered my son a percentage of the profits. I mean, come on, they are HIS toys!

When he had minimized all he thought he could, I decided to pick an arbitrary number. He has cars and wants to keep the cars...I let him decided which four cars he would like to keep. That gave him power, and he was able to make the choices. We got to the balls (and, I kid you not… he had balls from when he was a baby. I mentioned he's nine-years-old, right?), I picked a number and he narrowed it down to an appropriate, manageable number.

Interestingly, at first, he liked his new room. But, soon he felt it was too empty. He actually said, "I miss having my room full." We talked about that though, and he acknowledged that he didn't miss the chaos of having two full rooms, or the arguing to clean his rooms.

* * *

Tara has walked the walk with her child. She used creative thinking and made an impressive move with her downsizing. She is still purging and getting settled in her smaller home, but she has come so far.

* * *

Beth is a kindred spirit when it comes to decluttering and living frugally. She has been part-time at her job for about a year, and her family is doing fabulously! We get together and trade tips for saving money, reducing waste, and homesteading in modern times.

Beth writes (and this was edited for flow):

Raising children is never an easy job. Throughout the years, I have always said we were raising young men. We want to raise loving, caring, and responsible men. We want to raise men who value their families and contribute positively to their home and community, who will be an example to their own children of kindness and strength.

Teaching these values intertwines with the concept of contentment and other things described in Amity's teachings. Pressures in society have always existed. How one appears to others, and the bondage to other's opinions, can be overwhelming to people of all ages. Allowing our kids to participate in sports and activities with friends and have things they want and enjoy while still living within a budget is challenging.

Maintaining an organized home and guiding the desires and wants of our kids has allowed a unique pathway to teaching very valuable lessons of money management and responsibility.

Decorating a child's room can be extremely fun and satisfying to the creative endeavors of new parents. (It can also be expensive.) When the boys were little, the initial desire was to decorate each of their rooms in a detailed theme that our little boys would love. My imagination went wild as I anticipated all the fun things I could do in each of their rooms.

Then reality set in. Kids grow! They grow into young teenagers who don't want bright blue walls and dinosaur-themed wallpaper.

In anticipation of this inevitable, we choose to paint with colors suitable to a child at any age. We kept the dinosaur theme to the bedspread and had curtains made from fabric on sale. We chose to make simple tab curtains that could be washed easily and pulled open or shut by a young four-year-old. Shelving that could hold dinosaur figurines, Legos, or future books and sports trophies donned the walls.

For the furniture, an adult-sized dresser took the place of expensive toddler-sized furniture. Toddler furniture would have to be replaced in a few short years.  We went to an unfinished furniture store and painted an end table and head- and foot-boards in a color that coordinated with the room.  It was the fraction of the cost of Pottery Barn prices, and honestly, looked as good and was made as well.

Baskets labeled "cars", "blocks" or "Legos" kept toys organized and were placed on a book shelf's lower levels. Clean-up at night entailed putting the toys in their proper locations, and the boys learned to recognize letters from the description on the baskets.

Taking time with our kids to clean their rooms and teach them how to clean and organize was invaluable.  Roughly 5 -10 minutes an evening was spent focusing on their little world and instilling values of how to care for their things and take responsibility for their room.

As the boys grew and no longer played with some of their toys, we would pass them along to other young families and friends who had children. We always received compliments on how well-cared-for the toys were and even questioned if our kids even played with them!  Our boys loved their toys; and because they were taught to respect and take care of their things, the toys were in good shape and we felt good about sharing them with other kids.

Two to three times a year I would organize their rooms and go through their clothes. The older child's clothes were passed along to our younger child, until he was no longer small enough to wear them. Clothes that were too small for each child (and still in good shape) would be shared with a friend who had two boys several years younger than our own.

Toys the boys no longer used (and we weren't going to keep) were donated to our church's youth garage sale. Keeping track of their clothes and items allowed me to have an inventory of the items they would need as the year progressed. Identifying that the jeans no longer fit, or the long sleeves shirts were too small, allowed me to focus on the needed clothing items for the coming winter. No need to buy a bunch of shorts if it were October (unless I found a sale and bought larger-sized clothes for their future growth)!

We have always tried to focus on quality versus quantity. Christmas and birthday presents were limited to items the kids REALLY wanted. Our budget didn't allow for a plethora of gifts. However, we always made the effort to get them 2-3 gifts that we knew they would enjoy and had been dreaming of when making their lists.

As a rule, the gifts had to stay within the budgeted amount per child. If the item would consume a large portion of the budgeted amount, then the number of presents would be limited. The number of gifts wasn't equalized between children. We lived on a budget - only so much money was allotted for presents.

We were successful! The boys would spend hours and hours playing with their gifts. They never were deprived, and they usually received what they really wanted. They have consistently been grateful and appreciative of what they have received.

I remember when our oldest was turning nine. He wanted a very expensive Lego set. The cost of the set would result in being the only gift he received from us on his birthday.

He was absolutely thrilled when he received his gift! He played with it often and displayed the finished product proudly. He took care of it and showed my parents when they came to visit.

As the boys have gotten older, we have heard from relatives and friends what grateful children we have. They are thankful for what they receive and express their thanks openly. They have learned certain things are worth waiting for, and have demonstrated patience in purchasing items they want.

Saving money on meals with two growing boys has been another challenge. Budgeting for food has been an evolving budgetary item. Food costs fluctuate, and the amount of food each boy consumes in a day has increased!

It's always been a priority to give our kids healthy food choices. Growing them strong from "the inside out" has been so important to their muscle, bone, and brain development. Making their lunches a majority of the school week, while providing healthy food choices, is part of the daily routine. It saves money; and, in reality, the school lunches never provided enough food for our kids. They would routinely come home hungry at the end of the day if they had bought a school lunch.

Our kids are active and play sports. They burn calories and need the energy provided from healthy food to focus in school and in their sports. We avoided "snack packs" and packaged meals. Processed food is expensive, full of sugar and sodium, and provides little nutritional value per calorie. So, instead of the processed foods, we place apple slices or sandwiches in reusable containers that we wash at the end of the school day.

Another unique challenge (that we didn't have to deal with in our childhood) is travel sports. Our kids play hockey. In our town, there are only 1-2 hockey teams per age group. The community is not large enough to support multiple teams. As a result, we travel to other cities 3-6 hours away to play competitively. Hotel and food costs add up and are very challenging in maintaining a budget.

We have cut food costs by packing a large camping cooler full of healthy foods and drinks. We stay in hotels that offer breakfast, and try to stay in hotel rooms with microwaves and refrigerators. We can store our perishable foods such as yogurt, cheese, or lunch meat in the room's refrigerator and heat up some oatmeal, for example, in the microwave, to abate late night hunger pains.

We organize the cooler in the morning and stop by the local gas station for ice. Buying ballpark hotdogs or candy to "fill up" our growing athletes is not sufficient and usually results in stomach cramps. Racing to a fast food restaurant between games with 40 minutes to spare is stressful and hard on digestion. Instead, we find sitting in lawn chairs (under a tree, with our packed cooler full of nutritious food) is a nice way to relax between games.

We have also shared a hotel room with another family to split costs. My son and his good friend played on the same baseball team. My husband and the other boy's father got along well, and he and his wife were friends of ours. They would split the hotel fees and travel together, sharing the cost of gas. It was a nice financial arrangement for each of our families and saved several hundred dollars a weekend.

Sports equipment is very expensive. Our hockey association has an "equipment swap," where players can donate used equipment that no longer fits and pick up needed items such as shin guards or shoulder pads.  This is free, with the only stipulation that used equipment be cleaned and in good shape.  It's a wonderful way to rid our home of old hockey gear that no longer fits.  It has also been a very cost-effective way to start the kids playing in an expensive sport to ensure they had the appropriate equipment without spending a small fortune.

The equipment swap allowed them to play for the first year fairly inexpensively to see if they really liked hockey.  Sales and used sports equipment stores have been our "go to" in the boys' younger years.

As they have gotten older, their specific equipment needs are met a bit differently.  We won't "go cheap" on appropriate head gear and properly fitting skates.  But, at six-years-old, our young hockey or ball player didn't need to look like the pros.  They certainly didn't need to have a $200 bat or a $300 hockey bag.

It's important to keep the sport in perspective.  Expensive equipment doesn't make your child skate better, run faster, jump higher or get picked for a select team.  How your child looks is by far less important than how they feel about themselves.

Let them have fun and let them be kids.  Be present in their lives, show up for their games, and love them despite the score at the end of the game.

That's what matters most and that is what shapes their character.

Kids are under a tremendous amount of pressure these days to excel in sports. They are starting sports at younger and younger ages, and parents spend hundreds and thousands of dollars on camps and individual coaching sessions.

Never underestimate the value of a simple game of catch with your child played several times a week. Your young ball player would rather play catch with you any day of the week! That special time with your child is priceless.

A sports camp for a fifteen-year-old who has a desire to play his/her sports throughout high school may be a better distribution of funds than a seven-year-old who isn't as focused and still wants to play Batman or climb trees.

Climbing trees, walking across logs, jumping and running outside all support physical development and coordination in a young child. The outdoors are free, and fresh air and nature are good for everyone's mental health.

* * *

So, now you have heard from the pros. These ladies are rocking out simplification in their own families and have a lot of good advice to give. Take from them what you can, and apply it to your own family in your own way. They are happy to help.

Now that you have met my friends, it is time for you to meet the enemies of simplification. Up next are barriers common to the process, including sentimental items, just-in-case mentality, and the Joneses.

You are doing great! Keep going - you are on the home stretch now!

# Barriers

You can make tremendous progress with the right frame of mind. However, be aware that the path is often blocked by three dangerous adversaries: Sentimental, Just-In-Case, and The Joneses.

These adversaries will throw roadblock after roadblock for decluttering progress. They live to make you second-guess giving that broken clay pot to the dump, long after it has quit being useful and beautiful to you.

The first, and most common, is sentimental items. Everyone has things that hold deep meaning to them; but, when it stands in the way of being able to move with ease (or being able to maintain a sanitary, clean environment) it has become dysfunctional.

Sentimental is healthy and under good advisement in most cases. But, when it translates into not being able to let go of things, look closely at the underpinnings of that decision.

If you are having difficulty because of feeling sentimental, it may help to define, or redefine, what a gift is. Many people automatically default to the material good given as the gift, and the heart of the gift. But, let's look again at what a gift is.

An item is not the same thing as the person who gave it to you. It can be strongly argued that an item is not really the gift, rather, it was the thoughtfulness shown to you in the process of gifting you that was the real gift.

If you can separate the gift from the act of being given a gift, you can make real progress towards decluttering. No longer will the items need to stay. You will know that the item is wood, plastic, metal or some combination of materials, and the gift was the thoughtfulness, which will not fade with time, get damaged, or get stolen.

Long after the crazy-colored do-dad has left the building, the kindness that brought it to your doorstep remains. The kindness is permanent, sometimes even eternal, and will never fade.

If it doesn't bring you happiness, let the item go. If it is in poor repair, or not functional anymore, let the item go.

For those items that you still are attached to, but are willing to let go, take a picture of the item. That way, you can still have a visual reminder of it.

Just-In-Case is another enemy of decluttering. This is the extra five screwdrivers you have, the skinny jeans you never wear, and the cans of Pork and Beans that you have saved for the zombie apocalypse.

Just-In-Case can be fought with the reality that beyond a little preparation and supply, you don't need all the extra fluff. Have the jeans that fit you, now, in your closet. Don't buy food you wouldn't touch with a cattle prod (and I am talking about your canned meat collection). Let go of the extras of the extras in favor of one item that you will use consistently, and maybe one back-up. You will likely be able to buy toilet paper again. There is no reason to hoard it.

You need not get rid of everything except for 100 personal items, especially, if you run a house or an apartment. A little back up is not a bad idea. You can still simplify and not run out of milk or dishwasher pods. (I have an extra container of Cascade under my kitchen sink as this is being written).

Even yours truly respects Just-In-Case. I have survival food (a 30-day supply) and I have a water filter to turn a mud puddle into drinking water. I have two screwdrivers. I have one shelf of my linen closet devoted to… yes… toilet paper. It is far from overboard, however.

It's when the extra sundries get overwhelming and turn into clutter that action must be taken. You will know your own tolerance for things, but if you find yourself thinking "I might need that" and you own six of "that" take a pause, and unload that clutter!

The next enemy to decluttering is the Joneses. Not your literal neighbors, but those imaginary people in your head that you live to impress. The Joneses are the "they" that will think your car is so cool, your handbag so hip, or your vacation home so posh.

You may not want to change your life for fear that you will disappoint the Joneses. You may picture now their disapproving glances as you offload your son's baby clothes and tricycle (never mind the kid is 17-years-old) or roll around in a Beater-Mobile while you pay off your debts.

But trust me, you should seriously diss the Joneses. If you live free of their influence, you can do radically different than most in our society. You can get out of debt, build wealth at a rapid pace, or get your possessions to where they are manageable (and, maybe negligible).

Let's say you stop caring what other people think of you. You might be able to stay in your present home until you pay it off, or downsize into a smaller home and knock out your house-debt faster.

After you have paid off your home, credit cards (because the Joneses aren't telling you what you need to buy), and car loan, as well as every other debt, you can start building wealth.

All the money that went toward your debts is now going toward your investments and savings. Sound nice? It is! The rapid rate you can build wealth with no debt is astounding. You will quickly see your accounts rise with prudent investing and meticulous savings.

And, by not listening to the Joneses, you will sleep better at night knowing your nest egg is growing, growing, growing while you rest. You won't worry about getting the utility bill paid, nor having to put something back at the grocery check-out line.

Further, your house will get a lift and a lightening as you say "bye" to the nasty little Joneses in your head. You will stop bringing stuff you don't want into your house. You will decorate to impress yourself, not imaginary company. Likely you will choose to leave things out that have deep meaning to you, or a very important function (like a coffee maker and toilet paper).

Even though there are several stumbling blocks along the road to The Essential, it is well worth persevering and creating a new life with less stuff and more financial peace.

Now, let's switch gears and talk specific barriers to progress - those nasty money-sucking habits we all have. Come learn about seven habits - deadly to the wallet and the budget.

It's just beyond this page!

Take Action:

Keep what is useful and/or beautiful to you to be in your home. Dress to please yourself and be comfortable in fashions that you find appealing.

# Seven Deadly Sins for Simplifying

Adventure Shopping

Adventure shopping is probably the most dastardly culprit of wallet hemorrhaging because it is so subtle. What starts out innocently enough — "I have nothing to do this evening. I wonder what (insert store name here) has" — turns into three shopping bags and $90.57 on the credit card in a matter of minutes or a few hours.

Maybe it's our gatherer instinct pushing us to behave so madly, but something deep inside us propels us toward the cliff of financial imprudence. We have desires to escape boredom, sadness, anger, depression, and other emotions and we are told by our television sets, magazines, billboards, and internet pages that a slick something-or-other is going to make the discomfort go away.

My advice is, find some other way of getting your fix than at the mall or discount outlet. Find joy in producing rather than consuming. Create something instead, whether it is food for your family, a painting for your child, a game with cards, or something else entirely. Get outside if the weather is agreeable. Go for a bike ride or walk. Explore your neighborhood if you live in a safe area.

Cable

My husband and I have not ever had cable during our marriage. We have led happy, productive lives without the 60-ish dollar charge for tube entertainment. For the shows my husband wants to see that are on cable channels, we rent, or buy DVDs and we download. If you have 200 or more channels, can you really tell me you are getting your money's worth with a straight face?

Lattes

Lattes are addictive for sure. A 10-year, daily $5.00 latte habit is $18,200 over a decade! Most lattes and frappes are high calorie and high sugar. If you can make coffee at home, you will save a bundle.

Commutes

Commutes are killers to retirement plans. If your auto expenses are $10,000 per year, or an hour (or more) one way to work, you could be putting a $100,000 hole in the ozone every ten years. You could certainly affect when you can retire by having less in gas money spent, and less wear and tear (and subsequent replacement) of vehicles.

Eating Out

Restaurant food is not only detrimental to your waistline, but your wallet as well. The portions typically are enough to feed you twice, comfortably, or can be split between two people. When you eat at a restaurant, you can't control the food prep.

In my city there was a Hep A scare, and over 4000 vaccinations were ordered for those affected. Even if you fixed NY strip steaks at home you would not come close to spending what you would on many meals at a restaurant. By eating at home you have control over the cleanliness, ingredients, portions, and the expense.

New Vehicles

When you purchase a new, spiffy vehicle from the car lot, that "THUD" you hear as you roll off the lot is likely not your transmission, but it will very likely be a $3,000 or better drop on the value of the vehicle. This happens the moment you take it into your possession. So be smart, and drive used vehicles, where the brunt of the depreciation has already taken effect.

Gizmos and Gadgets

Electronic obsessions will getcha. Got to have the latest and greatest cell phone, iPad, TV, stereo? No doubt, if you are one of the first to get the device, you will pay premium, and the bugs in the system will be ones that you, and others like you, will discover and endure until all the necessary patches are issued. Let someone else do the beta-testing. Keep your money in your wallet until they come down in price and get the bugs fixed.

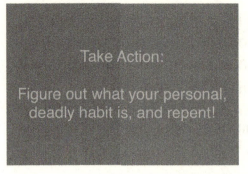

Take Action:

Figure out what your personal, deadly habit is, and repent!

Whew! A lot has been said. Thanks for making it thus far! Up next is the wrapping up and the final call toward a simplified, rich life. The wrap-up is in two parts, a personal example and a call to action.

Keep going, you are doing great.

# Life after Debt

Dave Ramsey is right. You can wander into debt, but you don't get to wander out of debt. Getting out of debt is methodical, and it is grueling. It is also so worth it.

A blogger that identifies himself as Mr. Money Mustache stated that a person needs to treat being in debt as though their hair was on fire. I couldn't agree more. It is an emergency. Your financial life depends on it.

The benefits to being debt-free are out of this world. When we were paying on our mortgage, I realized sometimes close to midnight that it didn't matter how up-to-date we were on our payments, we were always just a few months and some bad luck away from foreclosure.

Now that we have retired the mortgage, we know if we don't pay our rent to the government (in the form of property taxes) we would still be in a pickle. But, that pickle would take more time to materialize than a lapsed house payment. I rest easier at night, almost every night, with our new financial picture.

Not only do I have a sense of being ahead of the bulldozer, but I also have seen our wealth take off at a phenomenal rate. Just imagine if your house payment was suddenly put back into your pocket. How long would it take you to mass thousands or hundreds of thousands? It took us less than two years.

You can live on very low expenses, and live well. Some months we have spent less than $1500 total on our living expenses. We ate well - things like smoked and seasoned salmon, avocados, and New York Strip steaks. We also had gourmet coffee (from home) and our pets got the medical care they needed.

How did we do it? We didn't have a bunch of payments. No house payment, no cable bill, no expensive gym membership (ours is $10.76 per person per month). We don't have payments on flatscreen TVs, computers, appliances, or anything else large and depreciating in value.

We don't have expensive and space-hoarding hobbies. I don't scrapbook. I do have a sketchbook and I have a set of Prang watercolors to use (like elementary school kids have) when the mood strikes me. I don't buy a lot of books. When I buy books, they are generally used copies or e-books which tend to run cheaper than new hardbacks or paperbacks.

For entertainment, we work on our projects. I am now writing this manual (my fourth book) and my husband works tirelessly creating his video game with the help of a fellow

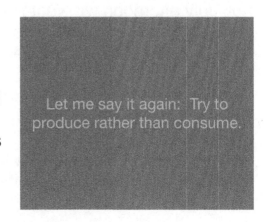

Let me say it again: Try to produce rather than consume.

programmer. We try to produce rather than consume.

There are all kinds of tips and tricks we use to keep our expenses low, and I will share those with you at the end of this book. But to get back to our topic - getting out of debt - it all depends on your attitude.

You have to get angry, nay, LIVID, about being in debt. Your nose must wrinkle in disgust at the very thought of taking on a monthly payment. You must hate writing checks to creditors and spit on your interest notifications on your credit card statements.

You must realize that debt is not a cute puppy. It is a Baskerville hound ready to devour you and burp up your bones. Debt is a killer of dreams and a good night's sleep. Better whack that thing upside the head a few times with some overpayments and the resolve to never be a slave to a creditor again.

You will be tested in your commitment to being debt-free. Our test came when my husband's car was broadsided on a thoroughfare in our city. In one hot, July afternoon we went from a two-car family to a one-car family. We were not prepared with our savings to purchase a new car. Not even a beater.

We discussed it and we decided to not get a car with a loan. This was a pivotal moment in our journey to financial freedom. We made do with one car for seven months. That was with blistering Missouri August heat and a bitter winter where I walked to work often so that my husband could take the car to his employment which was further away than mine.

Our grit paid off. We saved close to $10,000 during those seven months. In the end, my father let me know he was going to trade in his Hyundai Tiberon and I asked him how much he was going to get for the trade. He told me, and I gave him the middle of the range figure for the car. Since Little Red (the car) was a 2001 model, and the year was 2013, we walked away with a well-cared-for car and a healthy savings account. We still have Little Red today.

It's like the Heavens know you are trying to get out of debt; and you will be tested on just how serious you really are. I think it pays to make the hard choices and do without so you can avoid more debt, and so that you will put yourself closer to being completely out of debt.

And, I think, when the Heavens know you are serious about trying to get out of debt, you will get divine help. My parents were so good about pitching in and giving us spare food to offset our grocery cost. We were incredibly blessed that nothing major went wrong with our house, cars, or medical situation while we were paying double, triple, or even more toward our house.

* * *

Beyond the blood, sweat, and tears of the downsizing and debt-retiring process is a wild blue yonder. If I had known how my life would change for the better, I would have done my 20's differently (and even my teen years, too).

As I write this, I am sitting in my home with a damp head of hair from my shower on a Friday afternoon. I have not had to work since Tuesday. My husband and I spent some quality time at the gym this morning, and we also ran errands together, like recycling at our local waste center. I have made lentil soup and I am having a fantastic day, while most of the fellow city dwellers around me are chomping at the bit in their cubicles, anticipating a short, two-day break from work.

To start today off, I did not wake up with an alarm. My husband let me sleep until I woke up naturally and then we had coffee together on our living room futon.

I am still working, but just part-time. I work between two and three days a week on average. CJ works three days per week. I have been part-time for a year-and-a-half, and my husband joined me in part-time "employee-ness" for his company this past March.

We are not tight on money at the moment. The last several months that both of us have worked part-time we are still saving and are running in the black financially.

Our stress levels have dropped dramatically. Since I have been part-time, people tell me that I look well-rested. One dear friend let me know that when I was working full-time I always looked tired.

My husband also reports lower stress levels. In fact, it is kind of like I married another man! He is so much happier and more engaged in our marriage these days. He willingly helps with chores and cooking. He greets me often throughout the days and nights we are home together with little endearments. We run errands together and we do things like batting practice at a local park while most everyone else is at work.

We are not financially independent, but we are well-cushioned for most things that could come our way. If our course stays the same, we will perhaps fully retire in our early to mid 60's. But, because of our hard work and God's blessing, we are getting to enjoy a lifestyle of which others only dream.

So, is it worth it to stay the course? Is it worth it to partake in crazy spending fasts, media fasts, and shop at the bargain grocery store? I know my answer, and I know what benefits my answer and my subsequent actions have brought to me.

Every other week I get a five-day vacation. I don't get to spend it on a beach, but I get to do what I want to do without a boss telling me what I am going to do for those five days. Every other week, besides the other week, I get three days off in a row, and a bonus day on Monday to catch up things around the house. Do I need a beach to be happy? No. I need freedom, and I'll bet you are thinking much the same thing at this moment.

I am doing what I want to be doing. I don't want to retire fully right now. I enjoy the structure that work adds to my life. I enjoy having access to good insurance through my employer.

I am also enjoying creating this book for you. I hope you find it helpful and inspiring. Giving you the tools I used to find freedom brings me great joy and satisfaction. I sincerely want you to have the life of your dreams, with as few regrets as possible at the end of the time.

When you reach your essential and you recognize that you have enough, you are within reach of a magical experience: the realization that you can give.

In January of 2015, shortly before we retired our debt, I was coming to work. On this particular morning, I was rounding the corner in the surgical waiting area to go to my office, and then it struck me: there was nothing I wanted or needed.

All my Amazon orders were in; I had my wish list bought. Truly, I could not think of a thing I needed to buy. I felt like I had it all.

I remember feeling a sort of void. "What can I do now?" I asked myself.

"I can give." was the reply I gave my own heart.

And then, Minimize Ministries was born. It grew over the next few months and years. I offered it freely. I accepted no money for my time and I gave copies of my book away. It felt good. It felt blessed.

In January 2018, I decided to let go of Minimize as a name and adopted Simple Fly Life for the name of my project. It was simply a play on words - Simple Fly, or Simplify. Continuing in the tradition of a ministry, my goal with Simple Fly is to create a difference in people's lives and outcomes. If it makes money, that is fine.

Simple Fly is in its first year as this book is written. Time will tell how it develops and transforms itself and others. This is my dream, coming to life. I am truly living my dream life through simplification.

So, do I think you, too, should be debt-free? Absolutely! It is a hard path, but so worth it in the end. I recommend a debt-free, simplified lifestyle to anyone.

Start the journey today. Work hard and stay the course. You may be living your dream life sooner than you thought possible with the principles and tools outlined here.

And, I am not kidding.

# The Last Word

Our rising population on this planet is a concern to many. Some drastic measures have been put forward to control the number of life forms on this planet. Bear with me while I take you on one final rant.

* * *

When I see pictures of the planet - a little ball among twinkling lights - I fear for my quality of life among so many. But, as I sit in my house, or walk my neighborhood, I realize I am not a speck. I am a speck of a speck in the cosmos. The earth is enormous, and the universe is not fathomable.

Even though the planet is huge, and resources abound, I do not think that any of us are entitled to treat its bounty carelessly. I do believe it has enough resources to support all the life that is on it, but I don't believe that it will if each and every of the billions of us feel entitled to live the "American dream."

We are going through the resources available at an alarming rate. Each of us in the Western world need to scale back. Our greed is getting in the way of others' access to goods.

When we are a speck in the enormity of the problem, we don't feel responsible. But, collectively, we are making poor choices on how to live upon this earth. Our choices are creating divides and poverty for many. Our individual choices do matter.

The greed in our own hearts and the rise of discontent make us gnaw inside. The gnawing translates into shopping for many. We must change.

Future generations will likely need this planet. There is a Native American saying that says to the effect that the earth is not given to us by our parents, but, rather loaned to us by our children. We live in a closed system.

Figure out what it is that you need to survive. Leave a little room for a few wants and luxuries. Beyond that, strive not to consume.

Let's try to leave it better than we found it.

# The Frugal Way

(Adapted from Appendix D in <u>Minimize: Kill your debt. Live your dream.</u>)

1. Eat at Home: You will be amazed at how much you save when you cut out the burger joints and the Italian cafes. One month, my husband and I ate out a lot, and we ate out well. We spent $1200.00 on food out and groceries! That was just the two of us!

2. Meal Plan: It really helps to plan your meals. Take inventory of what you have in your fridge and pantry, and shop accordingly. Think about what you want to eat, and what you will eat. Go to the grocery store with a game plan, and stick to it once you are home. First, inventory what you have in your pantry area and your refrigerator. Think about what can be made (with what you already have) that you would actually want to eat. Then make a grocery list based on what you will need additionally to create these dishes that you have planned. By doing this, and do write it down (that is important), you will be focused on executing your plan and will be less likely to get takeout. By writing it down it becomes concrete, a reminder to you that Wednesday is taco night.

3. Batch Cooking: Have an afternoon or a day designated to undergo a cook-a-thon. By cooking large quantities, you will have the ability to use less energy, less of your time, and less clean-up to get your week's menu done. Just

make sure you have containers for smaller portions once your cooking is finished.

4. Buy Generic: That corn plant didn't know if it were going to be deluxe or ordinary. Neither did that cow think about to which dairy her milk would be going. Some things are okay to buy generic. With most things you will never know the difference. However, there are some things worth buying name brand. (Macaroni and Cheese is one of them.)

5. Buy in Bulk: This may sound contrary to minimalism, and it is, if you go about it the wrong way. For things that you actually need and use, it is fine to buy in bulk. I get fruit for smoothies, peanut butter, and canned meats this way. I consume it, and it is nice to have a stock on hand.

6. Eat Less Meat: Meat is expensive! I used to buy two tri-tip roasts at our local discount store. I stopped when I paid $28 for the duo. My husband and I have experimented with a more vegetarian diet lately. It hasn't done us any harm, and it's less of a gouge on our wallet. We make it a point to get enough protein.

7. Shop at Farmers Markets: I did this a lot last summer. I saved and had a lot of fun. My takes were delicious tomatoes, zucchinis, bell peppers, some meat, and baked goods. I felt good about

supporting local growers, and my husband and I ate like royalty!

8. Shop the Outside Edge of the Grocery Store: This is where the good, lightly- or non-processed, foods are. This is where you will find the produce section, the meat section, and the dairy section. Spend very little time in the inner aisles.

9. Shop With a List: So important! Decide what you are going to get before you ever set foot in the store. Stick to your list!

10. Shop Less: Shop for food once a week, once every two weeks, or for the really brave, once a month. You will spend less of your life in the store on trips to get a little something on your way home. You can shop less if you are willing to plan.

11. Don't Shop Hungry: Your body will send messages to your brain. A college friend told me she shopped when she was thirsty. She left with an obscene number of fruit juice bottles and not much else. Don't shop when you are vulnerable.

12. Price Match: When my mother was taking the paper she would bring the grocery ads to me. I scoured the ads every week, circling what I could use and writing the price, quantity, and item type on a piece of paper which would become my grocery list. I got loads of groceries

that might have cost $200.00 for around $130.00. My mom quit taking the newspaper, and I have not had much opportunity to get grocery ads since. I still have fond memories of hitting the jackpot on some items. I get so bent out of shape when I have to pay full price for cheese!

13. Refill Water Bottles: Instead of buying bottled water, buy an 8-pack of sports drinks and drink them, rinse the bottles, and refill them with tap water or filtered water. The chill they have once they have been in the refrigerator for a while replaces the slightly bad taste of the tap water. Reduce, reuse, and recycle this way - and save money. I use the water bottles in the house, and I take them with me when I am on the go, so I don't buy water when I am out. (Lately, I have purchased a glass pitcher to fill glasses from, and a fancy stainless steel thermos for hot and cold drinks for on-the-go drinking; and, I no longer purchase plastic.)

14. Buy Secondhand Electronics, Clothing, and Furniture: I have gotten some really good deals in the past with secondhand electronics. I buy from reputable sellers, and I choose what I am willing to buy. I got my iMac from a computer store in my city for less than half the price I would have paid new for the same computer. I got my bluetooth mouse from a seller on Amazon for less than $40 dollars; when new, they were $65. I would trust a store with a

return and exchange policy more than I would trust an individual, but you may be different. That said, there are bargains out there just waiting!

Clothing can be a great find as well. I have gotten some really quirky and fun t-shirts from Goodwill. I bought a pair of $120 designer name jeans for $25 at a Clothes Mentor store. In April of 2017, I purchased an entire spring wardrobe from Goodwill. Twelve items: $46.00! And I am happy with how they look! Like electronics, the deals are out there!

Furniture can be a way to get a good discount. I have bought a kitchen table and chairs second hand, a cabinet, and a wardrobe that I got much use out of (and for most of it I didn't pay very much). My mom is a pro at getting good deals on second hand items. Most of her furniture is from flea markets. She has an eye for matching and coordinating, and I love seeing what she does with her house, because it is interesting and she makes it classy.

15. Cut the Cable: Do you really need hundreds of channels to be happy in life? So, if your favorite shows are on cable, can you watch them another way, like - through the internet? My husband and I don't have cable, but my husband buys seasons of his favorite shows. He spends around $40 for a season and gets his fix. It's one less bill, and one less headache

to call about, if there is a problem with the subscription. (Now my husband uses Amazon Prime to get what he wants/needs.)

16. Unsubscribe:  Unsubscribe to magazines and newspapers.  Go online for news, or have a conversation with a friend or family member that keeps up with all that.  You will save money and reduce waste by doing so.  Like the pretty pictures?  Go to a library for magazines, or get online.  I don't miss out on celebrity gossip, because I read the headlines at the grocery store, and I look at interior decorating photo galleries online.  I don't feel deprived.

17. Batch Errands:  The more you can do at one time, the better.  Make a morning or afternoon for running your errands.  During the week, keep a list handy of what you need to do (but can put off), and add to it as needed.  When your designated time comes, look at your list and plan your route.  Sometimes, I even go so far as to list the things I want to do at that place specifically.  For instance, I might say, "Post office: Buy Stamps, Mail Package, Check PO Box.  Grocery Store:  Buy Groceries, Pay Utility Bill, Recycle Bags."  And, so on.  Play with your list and strategy until it works for you.  Just be efficient with your time.  Your gas budget will thank you.

18. Carpool:  If you live in the surrounding communities of a city and can find a buddy to

carpool with, you may save some serious money. Carpooling means two or more people are using the same resources to do the same task. You will save wear and tear on your car, as well as gas money, and perhaps have a relationship built because of the close quarters and time spent together.

19. Shop Insurance: My husband and I went to an independent agent to shop for insurance. We got a great deal on house and auto insurance, and did it all with one-stop shopping! We still have someone responsible for our account, but we can comparison shop at any time. (We use The Resource Center in Springfield.)

20. Turn Down the Heat: My husband and I turn our thermostat to 65 degrees in the winter. We have had it as low as 60 degrees during the time we were going to college. That is uncomfortably low for me. We have very reasonable (comparatively) utility bills in the winter, and we heat with gas! Even two degrees will make a difference. Go ahead, be brave, bundle up, and try it!

21. Hire a Competent Handy-Man: Mike, our go-to guy, is an asset! He does everything from hot water heaters to plumbing, to garage door openers, to electricity, to laying flooring and painting. He charges a fair price, too. If you can find someone who works well for you and

whom you trust, you can bypass expensive services when something goes amuck.

22. Fix Leaks: To my shame, I waited almost five years to fix a leak, because I thought it would be expensive. Turns out, the part was under warranty and was free! Don't put off doing something about your leaky faucets like I did. I cringe when I think of how much water I wasted, and how much our water bill was inflated because of my neglect.

23. Pay Your House Off Early: While you part with more money up front, you save a bundle in the long run. We have been paying on our re-finance for three years, and just now our principle amount is higher than our interest charge. We worked hard to get it that way. If you don't pay extra on your mortgage your loan source will get a bundle. Keep the money in *your* pocket (if you can), and don't pay hideous interest. (The house is now paid off completely.)

24. Double Duty Furniture: The house we live in is modest, and space is at a premium. Most of our furniture is not double duty, but our futon has been a life saver when we have had company. It doubles as a bed and our only couch. I have heard that trunks make good coffee tables, wardrobes make cool entertainment centers, and I bet you can come up with something even better than what is listed here!

25. Rotate Knickknacks: I would say this is for people in transition to becoming more minimal. Instead of buying more knickknacks, take half of your collection, hide it from yourself, and enjoy the other half until you are tired of what you see. Then box up that half, pull out the other half, and enjoy those pieces until you get bored and need a switch. The point is to stay out of the stores. If you really want to get minimal, stop buying knickknacks, get rid of yours except for a few, and enjoy the light work dusting is for you and how your wallet is padded.

26. Borrow, Don't Buy: Get to know your friends and neighbors! My neighbor has borrowed my lawnmower. My mom and I are constantly trading stuff, and my dad and I do much the same. My husband and I borrow yard tools and power tools from my husband's grandparents. It's just what you think: we take care of what we borrow, we return it promptly, and we are willing to return the favor. By not everyone's owning the same things, there is less waste, and more money in our pockets.

27. Accessorize: When you have a basic wardrobe, you can save a lot by spending a little on accessories. I have a few solid navy and black shirts that I spark up with one of three scarves, one of two sets of earrings, and different hairstyles. My scarves get lots of compliments; and it doesn't feel like I am wearing the same outfit over and over, though basically I am.

Accessorize basic pieces with a bit of flair. (Another thing to try is the Capsule Wardrobe, where you wear a few pieces for an entire season. This makes a person think through their wardrobe choices, and pick multifunctional, quality pieces over fast-fashion flimsies. I have done the Capsule Wardrobe from Fall of 2016 to the present.)

28. DIY Pedicures and Manicures: It helps to have a favorite girlfriend to do this with, but it can be done alone. Give yourself some personal time in the bathroom. Soak and maintain your nails on your hands and feet. Then get some quirky or elegant nail polish and take your time and paint your nails and toenails. I'll bet you won't spend 25 to 30 dollars, if you do it yourself.

29. Attend University Performances: For cheap, quality entertainment, check out the offerings of your local university. My friend introduced me to the wonders of a well done Chorale from the local University choir. We had a fun night, and it was free! We plan to do it again when we get the chance. Think also about sports events, art showings, and lectures for the community that your local University offers.

30. Rent at Home: Eighteen dollars vs five dollars to rent a movie is a no-brainer when you are trying to hold on to your money. Stay at home, pop some popcorn, sit with your fuzzy socks on, and save a bundle.

31. Explore Your Community: At one time I didn't know it, but my community has an Art Museum, Japanese Stroll Garden, tennis courts (open to the public), several parks, several libraries (with coffee shops inside them), swimming pools, and softball fields. What does your community offer? Take time to get to know the answer, and you may find things that cost little, or nothing, to enjoy!

32. Use the Library: At my library there are a coffee shop, copier, staffed reference desk, computers, and access to thousands of books, CDs, and DVDs. When I was in college, my study buddies, Teri, Nikki, Keiko, and I would spend hours on the weekends in the nice, private rooms studying. See what your library offers and stay out of traditional bookstores. If you have to delay your gratification, because of being on a waiting list, but you can read the same title for free in two weeks, it may be worth the wait. Same goes for DVDs and audio books.

33. Stay-cation: I have done this the last several years with great success. On my stay-cations I have explored the route I wish my employment to take, pondered life in general, and relaxed. I haven't gone from tourist attraction to tourist attraction, and wound up more frazzled and exhausted at week's end, than when I started. The home vacations have left me rested and

refreshed. When it is over, I have money in my account; I just don't have a wild tale to tell about pizza in Italy.

34. The Internet is a Tool: Question your internet habits. Would you be honest if you said you never shop or get ideas about what to buy next from being on it? I think the internet is best used as a tool for communication and information. I do my fair share of Google searches on it, but I get into hot water when I go on my favorite online retailer. You alone know your own limits and comfort level. Be respectful of your weaknesses, and make an environment in which you can thrive, and your wallet can remain intact.

35. Plan Your Christmas: My husband and I sat down the other day and listed everyone that we plan to give gifts. By their names we put the item we wanted to get for them and the dollar amount of the item. By doing this, we know what we are in for during the holiday season and there are very few surprises. Christmas expense does not sneak up on us. A tradition my husband and I carry out each year is one chilly day or evening, we layer our clothes, go to my husband's computer room, and shop for as much as we can on Amazon. We use our list and stick to it. I don't think we have done more than one Black Friday morning in our nine years (now 14 years) of marriage

36. Make Your Own Meat Broths: Recipes are easy to come by on line for vegetable, chicken, and beef broths. I store mine in a mason jar (don't fill to the top!) in the freezer until ready to use.

37. Do Your Own Car Washes/Vacuuming: This will save you on average 7 or more dollars each time you don't roll through the wash. If you live in an apartment, then seek out the cheapest place to wash your car. Cheapest one I know of in town is Blue Iguana. They are as little as 3 dollars with free vacuums.

38. Barter When Possible: I haven't done much of this outside my family. But, if I have been eyeballing my mother's knickknack, and she needs some help changing high light bulbs, we may work a trade!

39. Wait 30 Days: Wait about major purchases like TVs, computers, and vehicles. You may think better of it with a little time.

40. Drive Your Car to Its Death: I once made a blog post about how much we save per year by driving paid-for, older cars. It is a sizable savings to keep repairing a car that is worth $1000 even, rather than spring for a car loan.

41. Make Your Own Cleaners: It is amazing how much a few simple ingredients will clean. White vinegar is awesome, as well as Dawn dish soap. Look for recipes online and experiment

until you find a combination you like. I make glass stove top cleaner, granite cleaner, all-purpose cleaner, tub and tile cleaner, and glass cleaner rather than buying chemical cocktails at the store.

42. Use a Beauty School for Your Spa Day: If you go to a massage school, or a school that operates to teach the skills of facials, pedicures, manicures, etc., you can hit some good deals! I have had very relaxing massages and facials for as little as $10 through the one in my city.

43. Make Coffee at Home: How this saves money! Even if you get nice quality beans or ground coffee, you will be saving rather than going through a drive-thru for your coffee or latte every morning. Invest in a thermos if you are on the go for your go-go juice. Try to stay away from K cups - you can't recycle the single use containers from what I understand.

44. Compost and Recycle: By eliminating our wet trash (food waste) and our bulky containers (recycled) we have been able to switch over to bag service where we pay for our bags per year. We have seen our trash service bill drop by an average of 70 dollars per year, and we feel good about not trashing the planet.

45. Choose a Simple Hair Style: If you have all one length hair, you can choose to let it grow for as long as you want before getting it trimmed. I

have been known to get a haircut once or twice a year. If you pay 40 dollars once a month, that is $480. If you cut once or twice a year - that can be $80 total - that is $400 back per year. And, if you are willing to use a beauty school, you may pay as little as $5 per haircut!

46. Stay Out of the Stores: I have saved the best advice for last. Stay out of the stores. Let me repeat. Stay out of the stores! This is your best defense for not spending more than you should. I talk to myself as much as you when I say these things. If that special something doesn't get me when I walk in the store, it festers in me after I am home and I break down, go back, and get the item. When you stay out of these places you don't know what you are missing.

# The Playbook

(Adapted from Appendix A in <u>Minimize: Kill your debt. Live your dream.)</u> Revised for this edition.

## Living Room

Your living room may be a formal area, or a room that epitomizes its description as a living (lived-in) room. If you have a room that is the latter, I'll bet it could use some decluttering attention.

To start in the living room, do a sweep of the surfaces. Put everything into a pile if you are doing it all at once. Use your piles or boxes and try to make "Keep" the smallest. Re-shelve books that aren't being read, take magazines out to be recycled (or take them to Goodwill for resale), try to find all fifteen of your remote controls and put them in a central location.

Once you have your surfaces under control, go to your storage areas. Go through your bookshelves, your DVD collection, your CD collection (if you have one), and see what you can discard.

This is a place for tender honesty. Those books that we hang on to can be such a weight to us. In our culture, books are associated with being smart, and many books can look like a person is intellectual and well-read. I once thought this. It took a period of recovery to get past that feeling that I am what lay on my bookshelves.

If you are not going to ever read that book, or collection of books, again, let them go. Give them to the library, friends, or take them to a used book store. By all means, don't move the entire works of Shakespeare to yet another new home when you have no love for King James English.

DVDs can bring a bit of money if you take them to a trade-in store. My husband downsized his collection and we had grocery money for a few weeks from that. I also parted with the vast majority of my CDs that way. I hardly ever used them at home, and I did not use them in the car.

If you have a desk in your living room, that will need attention. Go through every drawer. If one of your drawers is a junk drawer you will need to deal with that.

Your coffee table may be a bit of a sore spot. It is where our keys, bags, and badges come to rest at the end of the day. Think about what is really essential for a coffee table. Before I re-decorated my living room, I had a coffee table. I had a single set of coasters on it as a permanent item. (Now, I don't have a coffee table!)

Try to think about what pieces of furniture you can part with. You should do this to your comfort level. For a long time I did not part with furniture out of my living area. However, as years went by, much of the furniture did a march out of my door.

Now, I have one couch, one easy chair, two ottomans, one floor lamp, a jute area rug, and a boot tray in my living room. I have a "floater" end table for my personal use that finds another place to be when company comes.

Think about how your living room functions. (This is a good exercise for every room in your house.) Think about what activities happen in this room, and try to accommodate those activities as best you can with your available furniture and belongings.

Do some maintenance. Change lightbulbs. Mend afghans and quilts. Launder throw pillow covers (consult cleaning directions first).

As you go through these things, clean. Dust your entertainment center's components, bookshelves, desk, and coffee table. Give the floors a good vacuuming or sweeping. Clean baseboards and windowsills.

Though these suggestions may sound laborious, I think they should be done. When you clean as you go, you foster feelings of connection and care for your dwelling. When you mend things, you connect with item(s) on a deeper level and you appreciate them. Whether you live in a mansion or a studio apartment, it starts to feel more like home when you put forth the effort.

## Bathrooms

If your bathroom is small like mine, space may be an issue. Your personal items may sprawl across your vanity. Our items do. We maximized our space before our remodel by using baskets hung with hooks on a towel rack. One for him, one for her.

After our remodel we had custom cabinets along one wall that really increased our storage area. Our vanity became a little larger and now we can comfortably put toothbrushes, soap, CJ's razor and shaving cream on the vanity without accidentally knocking anything to the floor.

We do store stuff on the back of our toilet. We do store items under our sink or in drawers. We have a linen closet in the hallway, adjacent to the bathroom, with our towels and medicines in it. It is not packed though, not even close.

To declutter your bathroom, start with surfaces. Start with the back of the toilet, shower caddies, or the stuff on your vanity. Remember your six piles and try to make "Keep" the smallest of all. Get your favorite cleaning solutions and clean as you go.

Try to make the surfaces basic. Maybe your vanity needs hand soap, toothbrushes, and a small basket to catch odds and ends. Question whether it needs three bars of decorative soap, a decorative hand towel (which is not the hand towel you actually use), and a ceramic fox for decor.

It is perfectly fine to do some maintenance at this point. Go through your towels and mend the ratty ones, or turn them into rags. Make sure your cold medications and prescription medications are up-to-date. Get rid of the ones that are expired.

Purge your make-up and your nail polish. Look online for guidelines about when to ditch mascaras, eyeshadows, and lipsticks. Allow yourself to have fresh contacts if yours are getting old, same goes with the toothbrushes.

Question whether you really need three half-full bottles of shampoo and conditioners. What about those beauty creams? Hair accessories? Part with what you can, and make a commitment to use the rest and get the containers out of your house.

I confess, I hit a super good deal on my favorite shampoo and conditioner, so I bought three sets of their 27-ounce size bottles. That is I, stockpiling. I have one bottle of hair mousse and that is the only hair styling product I have. I have a vial of black coconut oil that I use as perfume and I have another as back up. That is it on perfume.

I have been more lax about my makeup, but it fits in one small drawer along with all my hair stuff (one brush, one comb, and a few barrettes, ponytail holders, and clips). I have two bottles of lotion that I use in the house. I don't even have a bottle for my purse anymore.

For makeup, I like to get better brands. I do so because I can get quality products that stay on my face. I utilize the help of Kat, a beauty buff, who insists on going to the mall and getting professional advice in picking out products. Consequently, I do not experiment with different shades, types, etc.; and wrong colors and cheap products are not littering my house.

There is an exception to this that came about in 2017. I went on Amazon and knew what shades looked good on me due to experimenting long ago with Revlon. So I bought foundation, cover up, lipstick, mascara, eyeliner, and one container of eyeshadow from that manufacturer. I didn't have any duds, but I knew my colors, and I knew what would work.

Do what you can afford with make-up, skin care, and hair care. I get salon brands of shampoo and conditioner. Even though I have grown out my platinum blonde pixie cut, I enjoy the way Theorie products make my hair super soft (and I really like the fragrance).

You may be different. Don't get something on credit just because it was a good brand, but you don't have to go generic either unless you are doing it for financial reasons (like paying down debt). (And, I bought my entire stock of shampoo at nearly 50% off from Amazon's price at TJ Maxx.)

The same goes for body washes, soaps, and perfumes. You don't need several different kinds to make a functional bathroom. Think quality - without breaking the bank.

Set up a system of cleaning for this room. My system is that every week, at least once a week, I clean the toilet and the vanity. Once every two weeks, I give the tub a good cleaning. This way, it does not take a long time to touch up, and things never get atrociously dirty.

I am a firm believer in bleach tabs for the toilet. Scrubbing the toilet is one of my least favorite things to do. Bleach tabs really cut down on the need for this chore. The toilet has disinfectant in it, and the horrid ring around the waterline stays gone for months at a time.

## Kitchen

We are told that we need the latest gadgets, the most exotic spices, and the chef-endorsed cookware to scramble an egg. This is just not so. In actuality, a fully functioning kitchen can be had with much less.

One of my homies (CJ's term for my girlfriends) came over and we fixed breakfast in my kitchen. I will admit, we had to MacGyver a few things and come up with solutions, but we had a yummy breakfast of gourmet bacon and fabulous french toast with fruit. I love her to death, even though she called my kitchen "limited." But, "limited" fed us all with leftovers.

There you have it - a testimonial that you can cook well in a simplified kitchen. So now, we are going to minimize in this area. Are you ready?

Start with your big items. Are you still using your George Foreman grill? What about that food processor? Juicer? Slow cooker? Is your coffee maker built for 12 cups when you live as a single person and at best make 5 cups during the day? Your kitchen should fit your needs.

If you are not making macaroons and soufflés you may enjoy the space rather than extra dusting duty that your designer pans and baking sheets provide. You will be the best judge of what you use. I looked long and hard at my collection and came to terms that for the last five years I have not used my jumbo stainless steel skillet, therefore off to Goodwill it went. I gave my extra baking sheet to my father. (If I needed to borrow a baking sheet I know where to go.) I thought about what I cook, what I bake, and looked with honesty about how often I use pots and pans of various shapes and sizes.

Next, look at your dishes and flatware. Are you really going to serve 15 people in your apartment or home in the next year? Let go of the extra dishes, it will do you good.

At one time I had three sets, and that is not including a set of Christmas dishes. I had two sets of 4 settings and one set of 8 settings and a hodge-podge collection of Christmas-themed cups and plates. One set of 4 went to my father; the other set of 4 went to a friend because she knew of someone who could use them; the Christmas dishes went to my mom; and I now I just have the 8-place settings.

I went through my glasses and cups and got rid of roughly half, including the margarita glasses I never used. Then I got rid of the plastic cups completely and now use real glass glasses exclusively. I haven't missed my dishes, ever.

As you are going through your cabinets you can do a few things to help the process. I have heard it said, take everything into an adjoining room. I do not do this. Instead, I take a large bath towel, lay it in the floor beside me, and go cabinet by cabinet. The towel is a place to put the cabinet's contents as each item is scrutinized. I have been known to use bleach water and go over the shelves in the cabinets, getting dust under control and the invariable mess that finds its way into the cabinet space.

Next, go through your foods and spices. Check expiration dates on what is in your refrigerator and what is on your shelves. Part with whatever is out of date. I try to go through my refrigerator at least once a week to cull vegetables and dairy products that are past their prime.

Leading into spending fasts and frugality, use your once-a-week clean-out to coincide with menu planning. I strongly recommend this practice. When I use this practice, I have better luck staying out of restaurants and eliminating the event of wasting expired groceries.

For your counter space, just keep out that which you use every day. Try to put the little, numerous items like vitamin bottles somewhere else, out of sight. On my counter top I have a coffee maker, knife set, a pot brush, a steel scrubber, and hand soap, as well as a mason jar with bulk stevia powder. One hand towel floats around the kitchen, the rest are stowed away in a drawer. I do have much empty space on my counter top, and it pleases me.

In my home we did not have a dishwasher. I was the dishwasher for seven years. I know from experience, that it is possible to keep up with the dishes and not let them get overwhelming. I urge you to make it your practice to take care of your dishes at least once a day. It's less mental baggage when they are under control.

Wipe countertops and your table that you eat on at least a few times a day. There are few things that are as gross as feeling a bumpy, sticky countertop under my cleaning cloth.

Keep your tables clear of things like homework and mail. These surfaces should be available for eating. Once the homework is done, and the mail is sorted, those things need to find appropriate homes.

True confession: since I got rid of the desk that was in my living room, my dining table has become the command center of the house. My planner and daily sheets sit on the surface, as well as my name badge and my car keys. Need to find an alternative to this, and I will. I just haven't yet. (You have now been given the full disclosure.)

Mop and sweep your kitchen floors once a week, or at least every couple weeks. You will have a mental lift when your floors are kept clean. One winter (I am ashamed), I let my floors go for months. Trust me, you will thank yourself for putting out the effort to clean your kitchen area.

## Bedrooms

In my mind, a bedroom should be a place of calm, where a good night's sleep can be had with little effort. Things that take away from a bedroom's primary function can be many things. Some that come instantly to mind are computer desks, piles of books, and TVs.

Computer desks are workstations that attract clutter and are easy distractions from the more important task of sleeping. If possible, move the laptop and the desktop to another room.

The computer that you surf the net on before bed also serves to rob you of good night's sleep. When the first little problem occurs with casting off, and I reach for my MacBook, I can be found several minutes, to hours, later, browsing around on the internet. If I would just relax, I might get to sleep sooner.

Piles of books can be a detraction, too. If they are on your nightstand, they will be a reminder of what you read, or didn't read, as you try to go to sleep. Put your books that you read back on the bookshelf when you are done with them, or make your reading station in another room.

Seriously consider giving the TV (if you have one) in your bedroom a new home. TVs don't encourage you to sleep well. You get less sleep (and, reportedly, less sex), when you have a television in your bedroom.

Also, try not to eat in your bedroom. These are suggestions that work for me, and I feel that are worth mentioning. You may think of something else, or completely forsake my advice. No love lost. Just make it work for you.

Now that you have defined what your bedroom is for and what it is not, you are ready to clean. Make your list of nooks and crannies. If you are going to start small, pick some surfaces that can be cleaned quickly. The top of your dresser is a good one; also, nightstands work well to get a toe-hold of order in the room.

Once you have every surface under control, it is time to tackle the innards of your storage containers. You need to face everything. The bookshelf. Under the bed. Everything.

Empty a drawer and use your system of six piles. Everything in that drawer should go into a pile, with "Keep" being the smallest. Once you have a drawer empty, take a damp cloth and wipe out the drawer. Dry it, or wait for it to dry, and then put the "Keep" items in it, if indeed the "Keep" items go there.

If you are able, empty a piece of furniture entirely at one time. Empty the chest of drawers, the trunk, the nightstand, and anything else you may have. Use your piles or boxes and clean everything at once. If you have furniture polish, and it is appropriate, give it a good once-over before you start putting your "Keep" items back.

For the surfaces, opt for not much clutter. Two or three items total should be what you aim for on your surfaces, if that.

When you are cleaning out, try to clean as you go along. It takes more time, but there is something charming about knowing that not only are you decluttering, but tidying, too.

If you haven't lately, take your sheets and blankets to the laundromat, or your own laundry room. You may want to splurge for quality laundry soap and fabric softener. I recommend sleeping on fresh, good smelling sheets when you can come by them.

I grew up with bed sets that were frilly and had multiple pieces. Recently, I took a long, hard look at my habits, and I had to admit that I enjoyed the beauty of a well-made bed, but being able to straighten it in about 20 seconds was far more appealing to me at this juncture of life. Make your own decision, but feel free to be open to possibilities other than what you have previously considered.

If you are tempted (as I am) to put things under the bed, consider this: You will know you have clutter under your bed in your newly minimized home. If you must use that space, I recommend organizers (yes, I said organizers) to make it easy to pull out from under the bed so you can get to what you need. Preferably, you will declutter to the point that you won't need to have things under the bed.

## Closets

Closets are a blessing and a curse. They bless, by giving you a space to put items not in use. They curse, by giving you a space to put items not in use.

I have owned walk-in closets; and, currently, I own a 30-inch wide closet. My wardrobe has adjusted accordingly. If you have a large closet, it is important that you face it, and that you consider that just because the space is there does not mean you need to fill it.

Your closet space should be useful to you. This is an area where most of us need to declutter, and after decluttering, should probably organize as well.

For your clothes, turn hangers backwards when you are done wearing an item. Do this for about a month. Then you will have an idea what items you are actually using.

For your shoes, put an index-sized note card in one of the shoes in each of your pairs. When you wear the shoe, take the note card out. In a month, it will be easy to know if you are wearing those precious navy pumps or not, depending on the presence, or absence, of the note card.

Most of us have more than shoes and clothes in our closets. Deal with all of it. Question each item:

- Do I use this?
- When did I use this last?
- Is this benefitting me?

Put in one of your piles accordingly.

In my closet, I have less than 10 pairs of shoes including rain boots, snow boots, a dressy pair of boots, one pair of flats, two pairs of athletic shoes, one pair of flip flops, one dressy pair of sandals, and one thrift store pair of off-brand Uggs. I have a shoebox of cards and letters from my loved ones and some eye glass cleaner. I also store my sewing machine in my closet, and two quilts that my grandmother and great-grandmother made.

It is possible to get a wardrobe under control to the point that clothing from all seasons fit into the space at one time. It is possible to downsize to 10 or 15 pairs of shoes total (which is generous), including house shoes.

Once you get done decluttering, it is time to organize. Put your clothes together in a way that makes sense to you. You may decide to organize by color, season, or function (or all three). If you don't have a shoe rack, I recommend getting one, and it pays not to buy the cheapest solution out there.

My shoe rack fits in the bottom of my closet. It reminds me of shelves at a shoe store. The front is slanted so the heels of the shoes are higher than the toes. If you have a specific place for your shoes, then you are more likely to put them back in the same spot when you are done wearing them. They are easier to find on the rack than in a pile at the bottom of your closet.

Above all, do what you know will work for you. It may be helpful to have some plastic bins to store loose stuff. Fine. Just remember that you are still responsible for it as long as it resides in your home.

The coat closet needs the same kind of attention as your regular closets. So does the linen closet. Take on a closet a day, or a walk-in closet over a weekend stretch, until you get it conquered. You will be so glad you did.

## Wardrobe

My personal wardrobe has been an evolution, as I bet yours has been. Once upon a time, I felt like I had to dress a certain way so that people would believe certain things about me. I had cute dresses, several pairs of heels, and fat and skinny jeans.

Over time, especially when I entered my 30's, image became less important. I found myself seeking what I felt comfortable in, and picking quality over fashion.

Once I filled up a walk-in closet with my clothes. Now my clothes are stored in one part of a wardrobe cabinet, 5 bottoms and 10 tops that are dressy hang in my closet, and three drawers hold my underwear, socks, shorts, and other miscellaneous items. My clothes fit me, feel comfortable, and (for the most part) are quality made. When they don't fit, feel great, or can't be mended by me, they find a new home.

Less clothing means that you wear what matters to you, and you really *wear* what matters to you. Now, nothing sits at the back of my closet wrinkling, and surprising me months down the road when I realize I still have that, whatever it is, lingering in my possession. My clothes are used frequently, and I feel like I get a good value out of them.

Like most-things-minimal, wardrobe changes are a process, and a personal process at that. It may take weeks or months to come to terms with where you are size-wise and style-wise. Have patience and persevere.

After a few weeks or a month, it is time to go through and assess your closet. Take a hard look at what you are not wearing. Try to re-home as much as possible.

This purging happens for most through multiple attempts and exercises in throwing out unusable/unworn/unsuitable clothing items over months or years. Give yourself time to get there, and be honest about what you are actually wearing. Discourage a "fat" wardrobe and buying clothes that don't fit now as you hope to shrink into them.

Do purge on a frequency. At least at the beginning of each season and at the end of the season. Relieve yourself of things you have no intention of wearing, and things that, as time has shown, you aren't wearing. Donate them, give them to friends, sell them, but do not house them any longer than you have already. Don't delude yourself into thinking that you may wear it again.

Take a hard look at what you are wearing. What are the trends you see? Do you like flats? Scarves? Do you gravitate toward dresses or pants? See what you like to wear, and shop in the future accordingly.

Be honest with yourself. Do you really need ten black skirts? Do you really need that cocktail dress or that business suit for your lifestyle? What about those sequined shoes...how many outfits can you wear with them? You may not be able to part with clothing down to 33 items, but what about picking your four favorite skirts and part with the rest?

The minimalist has fewer clothes on average than the regular consumer. I find the following philosophy especially useful with clothing: Think quality not quantity. It goes something like this: if you can buy ten shirts for 10 dollars each, or get five shirts for 20 dollars each that are well made and fit properly, you may do better to get the more expensive shirt for a few reasons.

The shirt will bring you greater satisfaction. You will feel better and more put-together when wearing it. If it is a flattering fit, you will get compliments on it. You will feel more confident in it, also.

The shirt will likely last longer. If it is quality made, the shirt will keep its shape, be color-fast, and will be easy care. Who could complain about that?

You will have fewer shirts in your wardrobe. I have heard it said to stick to a base color, or two, for your wardrobe. Since I started the capsule wardrobe, I chose black as my base color. I have a few denim pieces, but by and large my clothes are black, gray, and white. I have one pair of khaki capris.

This is not to say it is time to throw away all your clothes and shop at the most expensive place you know. It is a process that for most of us, must be done gradually, secondary to budget restraints, and just a general sense of not wasting clothing.

I shop for clothes at thrift stores. I try to shop twice a year and no more. I make a list of the items I am looking for and make sure I have an entire afternoon to devote to hunting. That way, I can get a brand new (to me) wardrobe for each new season. I don't break the bank, and I get what I want - or in the neighborhood of what I want - much of the time. I frequently can find my favorite brands at a fraction of the original cost. Rarely, I will buy a piece online.

When starting out on minimizing your wardrobe, adopt a 1-in/2-out rule. This means if something comes in, two like items must depart. Stick to this rule and in a shorter time you will have your closet under control.

These days I have a 1-in/1-out rule. When in 2013 I got six t-shirts, I packed up six old t-shirts and took them to Goodwill. The t-shirts that took residence in my home were black or navy, well made, and on sale. The six that left were ones with holes in them, distortions in the fit, or stains.

I purge my clothes after each season. I try to put limits on what I have so I choose to have 5 nice bottoms and 10 nice tops total. I do have loungewear and everyday shirts - so don't think that I just have 15 pieces of clothing.

Keep at it, progress will come!

# Garage

In 2013, cleaning out our garage was a family affair. It took my husband, my mom, and me the greater part of the day, and it was a detached, one-car garage.

For years I had been moving things out of my house and into the garage. Cardboard boxes and old papers were to be named, among other things, that went to make up the mess that was adjacent to our house.

This past spring, I did a very thorough clean-out of the same garage. This time I did it myself, and I did it in two hours. Are you ready for this? I had enough stuff that I cleaned out this last time that it lined the outside wall of my garage back to our shed, and the cast-off items stood out as much as five feet away from the wall. We had wood scraps, water-damaged luggage, and paint from our remodeling that didn't make it past the eagle's- eye test for clutter.

When you are cleaning out, I think it is very appropriate to use your garage as storage for things that eventually are going out the door. I don't think it does well as a place for things for an indefinite period of time which don't otherwise have a home. I still use the garage throughout the year for a dumping ground of things I am not sure I want to let go of yet. Every spring though, I deal with it, and the garage gets a clutter facelift.

To start cleaning the garage in 2013, my husband and I waited for a sunny day. We pulled everything out of the garage and began to sort through our stuff. When we had everything pulled out, we swept the floors and got the big cobwebs down.

We created piles that were meaningful to us. We had a pile for cardboard boxes. (My years of online shopping gave us a wealth of boxes and packing material.) We had a pile for tools. We had a pile for camping gear.

We had a debris pile. The debris pile had iron railing, concrete pedestals, rocks, bed rails, and more. Remember this, because I will refer back to it in a minute.

Then we began labeling and boxing things. We had bought packing tape, a large Sharpie marker, and uniformly-sized cardboard boxes for the occasion.

We boxed up the loose tools and the gizmos. My mother patiently inventoried and stuck a copy of the inventory of what was in the box on its side. When my husband was done culling his tools, we were left with four boxes. We stacked them up in the corner of the garage.

We used existing shelves to our advantage. We did not buy organizing items other than the boxes to clean our garage. We took everything down from the top of the garage and tried to keep it from ascending again when we were done cleaning.

The things out of the garage that you are going to get rid of need to be dealt with swiftly. If you have charity things, call a charity that has pick-up service, or load your vehicle and take everything to the charity the day you clean your garage. I had to put my charity items back in my garage temporarily. I gave them their own space, and I wasted no time in calling our local D.A.V.

Ideally, if you are having a garage sale, the sale will take place the following day. If not then, try for the following weekend. Do not delay.

For items that need a new home, take care of them promptly. Call your family members if they have items stored in your garage that you don't want to have in there. Ask them to get their stuff. If you must, get brutal and say it is going on the curb, or in the charity bucket, in a few weeks if they don't claim it. It is up to you if you want to follow through on your threat or not.

Now, if you will remember our debris pile, it is time to make some phone calls. For my situation of the things that belonged in a landfill or recycling center (that I did not know how to contact) I called 1800 GOT JUNK. For $92 they took everything, even yard waste, and promised to recycle what they could. I used them a second time this past spring, and I had a coupon which offset the cost considerably. Their sale notices are one of the few emails I like to see in my inbox.

It was worth every penny. Concrete planters, PVC piping, and construction materials went away from me forever at the same time in 2013. The wood scraps, paint, luggage, cardboard boxes of unusual sizes, and moldy baseball equipment left this past spring. It was a really good feeling to have it hauled away, never to be haunting me again.

Decluttering should go into the final frontiers of your property. Once you get done with your home, do the garage, shed, basement, and attic. Your workspace could use attention, as well as your vehicles. Get through it all, and be lighter and merrier.

More From Amity's Other Books…

From <u>Minimize: Kill your debt. Live your dream.</u> Published in 2013.

We will be exploring Minimalism as it pertains to stuff in great detail next. However, now it's appropriate to introduce the meaningful differences in the two concepts of frugality and Minimalism.

Frugality and Minimalism are very closely related, but have some fundamental differences. To define frugality, it needs to be made clear that frugality is primarily about saving money. Through thrift, frugality cuts expenses.

Minimalism, on the other hand, is primarily about simplicity. Minimalism deals with many more aspects besides money. Saving money, however, is a byproduct of that quest for simplicity. Making do with what one has, rather than buying the cheapest item to fit the need, is a big contrast between the two philosophies.

Both philosophies encourage fiscal responsibility. Minimalism encourages good stewardship by buying what is needed. Doing what it takes to fill the need may not be the cheapest product. A cheap solution might serve the need for a time, but to get the best price to value ratio from a purchase you may need to think higher quality and, therefore, higher price.

For instance, if lawnmower A is $150.00 and lawnmower B is $250.00, you may be inclined to go with the cheaper option. However, when you consider that lawnmower A's life expectancy is three years and lawnmower B's is seven years, lawnmower B winds up being less cost per year, even though initially the price is higher.

Both concepts discourage impulse and recreational shopping. Minimalism encourages a decline in consuming overall. The reasons for this can be from saving the planet to sparing your wallet. Frugality encourages reducing expenses through thrift and responsible shopping.

Minimalism is not necessarily frugal. It is not about getting the cheapest shirt; rather, minimalism is about owning a minimal quantity of quality shirts that are adequate for your lifestyle. You can drive a new car and be a minimalist; and you can spend money on tickets to movies without a twinge of conscience.

Frugality is about getting the best deal possible for the least amount of money. If it weren't at a discount, it wasn't a good find. Paying full price is a mortal sin, and the thrill of the bargain beckons the frugal person to sometimes buy ahead.

Which concept does the best in my opinion? Both are excellent, and will be applicable in most situations. I like that Minimalism strives for simplicity; because, under frugality, if you can buy a package of bathroom tissue for ten cents, it's okay to buy 200 packages. Hoarding may become a habit if self-monitoring is slack.

While it's good to enjoy having "enough," stockpiling against the dreaded (but highly unlikely) day that you might be out of toilet paper (and there is not a store within 75 miles that has some), is definitely against minimal principles. If you choose to stockpile, you have a load of money sunk in toilet paper that could be earning for you in a savings account or other money maker. If there is a better deal down the road, you'll miss it, Your storage space is loaded, so another good deal for another type of product has to be foregone.

I like it that frugality is about intelligent consumerism. Frugality researches purchases and strives to get the best deal. Where I depart from being a devotee is when the hoarding tendency raises its ugly head.

I also depart from minimalism when "extreme" simplicity raises its head. Thirty-three items in a closet is not feasible for me. Neither is going without a car. I enjoy having options when I face my closet in the morning. I feel good about spending my money on transportation that is convenient and affordable for me, since it saves time and occasional weather-related distress.

What I would like to strive for is reasonable, frugal (moderate) minimalism. Moderation, I have found to be a friend in my life. Philosophers have suggested it as a way of life that can lead to happiness. Happiness is the only virtue that is pursued for itself, according to Aristotle. I do want to strive for simplicity in my life, and I enjoy saving a buck or two.

For more, read <u>Minimize: Kill your debt. Live your dream.</u> Available on Amazon.

Made in the USA
Monee, IL
29 April 2022